HAROLD MONRO

COLLECTED POEMS

HAROLD MONRO

HAROLD MONRO

COLLECTED POEMS

EDITED BY ALIDA MONRO

WITH A PREFACE BY

RUTH TOMALIN

DUCKWORTH

First published 1933 by
R. Cobden-Sanderson Ltd.
This edition 1970
ALL RIGHTS RESERVED
Preface © 1970 by Gerald Duckworth & Co. Ltd.
3, Henrietta Street, London, W.C.2

SBN 7156 0527 5

Printed in Great Britain
by Photolithography
Unwin Brothers Limited
Woking and London

PREFACE

by RUTH TOMALIN

HAROLD MONRO was both poet and practical idealist. By a stroke of good fortune, as he said, he was expelled from school at sixteen. Cut off from other companionship, he discovered Byron, Keats and Shelley. Defiantly at first perhaps, then with a growing sense of vocation and apprenticeship, he ranged himself with the poets, and devoted the rest of his life to poetry.

As a young man he often wanted only to live in solitude and write, but he felt that a poet owed more than this to the community. So he founded a bookshop in London to find a wide audience for poetry—which, in the early years of this century, had even less prestige than usual in England. His venture was successful, and he came to have great influence; yet he feared that he had betrayed his own gifts. The conflict between two aims became a torment to him, driving him into a private wilderness of stress and illness. From this "bitter sanctuary," at the end of his life, he wrote his best work.

His friend F. S. Flint, the Imagist poet, described that conflict as he saw it: "Harold Monro was a dark Scot, and from the complication of that ultimate origin flowed both his virtues and his vices both as a man and as a poet. All his adult life he was haunted, the wild Celt in him at odds with the thrifty heir of a line of cautious physicians. He was a living contradiction in terms, not only (perhaps less) as a poet and shopkeeper, but also in everything else. It is hardly possible to state one of his characteristics without immediately being reminded that in him too was its opposite. He was hard-working and lazy; he was generous and mean; he was a lover of freedom and a tyrant; unconventional and conventional; a bohemian and a bourgeois . . ."

Towards the end of Monro's life, Humbert Wolfe wrote of the great debt that the new movement in verse owed to him. For poets of his day, said Wolfe, the Poetry Bookshop had been the Mermaid Tavern, and its founder a source of inspiration. Where others had merely talked of their art, he had "quietly, without profession, lived for it."

He was born in Brussels on March 14, 1879, and spent his early childhood there, going on to a preparatory school at Wells in Somerset, then to Radley and Caius College, Cambridge. His father, an engineer, came from a family distinguished in medicine, to which Harold Monro's son would return.

According to Flint, "like many other men who afterwards became famous, he was a rather dull and stupid boy at school with an aptitude for getting into mischief or into the position of scapegoat." He left Radley in disgrace, apparently because bottles of wine were found in his study; and it is easy to see what a shock this episode, with its aftermath of aimlessness and family disapproval, must have been to a reserved and sensitive boy. He saw himself as a solitary and wayward youth, slow and dreamy, unable to stick at anything for long. But already he was finding his own way. "Safe away from school," he read Virgil for the first time with enjoyment, going on to discover *Childe Harold*, *Endymion*, Shelley, Milton and Tennyson. He read the *Hymn To Intellectual Beauty*, and Shelley's dedication became his own. He began to write poems and stories secretly in his bedroom, filling copybooks as fast as he could buy them.

By the time he went to Cambridge, in 1898, poetry had become an obsession, though still in secret. In his third year, however, he formed a group with three other under-graduates to read and criticise one another's verses; his first experience as adviser to other poets. He read modern languages, and while spending six months abroad he became absorbed in French and German poetry. After taking his degree he studied half-heartedly for the Bar—"but I usually had *Paradise Lost* or Keats open on my knees or in my Justinian." The habit of taking long walks, begun in Germany, was continued in London: "I developed the habit of writing my verses at night, and I walked by various round-about ways back home every evening, preparing myself for the night's work and repeating my verses over and over to myself with the object of improving them."

Giving up law, he married in 1903, when he was twenty-four, and worked for several years as a land agent in Ireland. For one of his background and temperament a more un-suitable post could hardly have been found, and the marriage too was desperately unhappy. His wife was a sister of Maurice Browne, one of the men with whom he had discussed poetry at Cambridge, but her talents lay in another direction: she had had the distinction of playing hockey for England. During the engagement both had realised how little they had in common, but failed to free themselves. Isolated in that rainy melancholy countryside, he found the whole situation driving him close to suicide. In 1908, after one of several partings from his wife, he was writing bleakly: "So I have to make up my mind and resign myself. It was my aspiration to be a real poet. But now for the folly and obstinacy of my early youth I must atone. Why did I surrender my dear dear freedom?" Significantly, a month later he recorded: "Dreamed that at last I gave way to the drink fiend and fell right into the habit."

But he did not resign himself. His private means made it possible to escape, to walk about Europe, spend a year or so alone in the Swiss mountains, to try out various social theories by living in "crank settlements," to walk from Paris to Milan in the spirit of Hazlitt and Stevenson, and to write a long essay about it in the prose style of lesser writers. By 1910 he was living happily in Florence, in a circle which included Charles Tennyson, the novelist Maurice Hewlett and a young student, Arundel del Re, whose enthusiasm for poetry must have recalled his own at that age. Dr del Re, now a lecturer at the University of Melbourne, writes: "Monro had a pleasant oval-shaped face with a high forehead and a rather large nose, nice eyes and a quiet reassuring personality that at once set me at my ease. The study smelt agreeably of tobacco; the walls were lined with books; a Bar-Lock typewriter—which later was to be my faithful enemy when it became the editorial typewriter in the offices of the *Poetry Review*—lay on the desk covered with papers but, so it seemed to me, very tidy for that of a poet. I curled myself up in a deep armchair in front of the fire and plunged straight away into the subject of poetry and discussed Keats, Shelley, Carducci and D'Annunzio. Then Monro started to read aloud in his soft yet clear musical voice. It was my first experience of the kind and I have never forgotten it."

Monro, he found, was "a scholar and philosopher, but not an intellectual: not a bit romantic, though an idealist. He taught me to love poetry. He was also very keen on music, though he did not play, and many nights he and I went to chamber concerts or to the opera. At weekends we took his cocker spaniel for walks in the country round Florence." Like Keats, they stayed for a time in a mill-house, "an island of greenery with nothing but the sound of hidden water and the wind in the trees." Here, at Ascona above Lake Maggiore, Monro entertained his friends and corrected the proofs of his third book of verse, *Before*

Dawn. Two earlier books—a collection of youthful verse on classical lines, and a long poem, *Judas*—had appeared respectively in 1906 and 1907. The new collection contained experiments in social satire, expressing his discontents with the world and the drabness of most men's lives. This social concern was genuine, and Shelley's idea of service to the community had always appealed to him. His conscience would not let him drift indefinitely. Now it spurred him on to attempt something practical in his own sphere.

It was Maurice Hewlett who gave him the right impetus. Monro had been complaining about the state of English poetry, which, so far as it had any place in the public mind, was associated with the effete and precious; a legacy from the 1890s which Monro, despite some lapses in his own work, would fight all his life to destroy. The poetry of the future, he told del Re, must express the ideas and feelings of a new age which was dawning, an age in which man "must begin to live life more joyously and rationally."

Flint wrote: "Hewlett, in his forthright way, exclaimed, 'If you feel like that, for God's sake go back to England and do something.' It was a turning point in Monro's life. Hitherto, Shelley, vegetarianism, romantic idealism, a vague socialism and his own fundamental incapacity to submit to discipline had rendered him ineffective both as a man and a poet. He was to learn about men by the experience of them which money dealings give, and about poetry by the lash of other poets' tongues."

He returned to London in the autumn of 1911, and in little more than a year, by sheer drive and enthusiasm, coupled with the authority of his critical work, he had become a leading figure. In 1912 he was to Edward Marsh "the obvious person to approach" as publisher for a crusading modern anthology.

His first plan was to edit a periodical, and the monthly

Poetry Review was launched in January 1912. Del Re, who had come with him from Florence, writes: "Monro leased a cottage in Essex, The Old Malting House. I was acting as assistant editor, and on Saturdays I would collect my salary in gold sovereigns and after a hurried lunch at the Bodega in Fleet Street we rushed to catch the train for Bishop's Stortford. The weekends were busy, reading manuscripts and poetry and planning the first issues of the Review."

Its function was to be mainly critical, but contributors of verse included Rupert Brooke (with *The Old Vicarage, Grantchester*), Flint, Flecker, Padraic Colum, James Stephens, Ezra Pound: "Pound's individualistic and a trifle doctrinaire attitude towards poetry made him sometimes impatient with Monro for his very Shelleyan conception of the poet's function, but he acted as a powerful stimulus to Monro, and, together with Flint, and, to a lesser extent, T. E. Hulme, encouraged and backed the venture as soon as it was started."

Monro had rashly agreed to edit the paper in alliance with the Poetry Society, but a year later he extricated himself to found his own quarterly, *Poetry & Drama*. For his office he had taken an eighteenth century house, 35 Devonshire Street, off Queen Square in Bloomsbury. Now it occurred to him that a great mass of new verse was being printed which would never be heard of—let alone bought and read—by the public. What was needed, in fact, was not only intelligent criticism, but a shop to specialise in the sale of verse, run by someone who really knew what he was offering. In January 1913 he opened the Poetry Bookshop.

Monro's views on what he was doing were admirably clear-sighted. In an article that spring he wrote: "Poetry cannot be forced into popularity, but it can at least be given a chance; and I conceived the ambition of providing for the public an opportunity for testing, without difficulty and of its own initiative, this extraordinary thing it pretends to despise. But the less written about it the better, and the less of it printed the better; and the more it is carried in the memory and conveyed by the voice, much, much the better."

The house in Devonshire Street was to be a centre for poets and the public. The shop was a small room about twelve feet square, furnished with homely oak tables and settles, lined from floor to ceiling with books—poetry old and new, plays, essays, lives of the poets—and hung about with gaily coloured rhyme sheets, which also lined the window. For a few shillings, Eric Gillett recalls, "one could buy enough to decorate a small room with broadsheets of poems by de la Mare and others, gleaming with Lovat Fraser's lovely colours." The door opened on to a narrow dingy street, given over, Osbert Sitwell found, "to screaming children, lusty small boys armed with catapults, and to leaping flights of eighteenth century cats"—was he thinking of Hogarth's ferocious nursery tabby? Approaching customers were in danger of being hit by kipper skins and other rubbish tossed from windows. This does not sound altogether inviting; but the idea of a bookshop in a slum had its own attraction, though not for the neighbours, whom Monro had hoped to benefit. He thought, said Flint, that he would be bringing poetry to the people, "but the people cared nothing for poetry, and the acquaintances he made in Devonshire Street merely regarded him as a possible source of free drinks after the public houses had closed": while their children, given some attractive prints, tore them up and stamped on them, preferring catapults and hopscotch.

To outsiders, however, the setting was novel and romantic. Much of the street was occupied by goldbeaters, and the thud of hammers sounded there all day. Inside the shop, the atmosphere was peaceful and welcoming. Visitors felt free to browse without buying, or to ask advice. Among those who did so was a wealthy man who needed someone to inspect his furnishings, before ordering whole shelves of classic poets specially bound to tone with his colour scheme. Another came in search of a book for her sister, a "very poetic" girl of seventeen. Offered *Peacock Pie*, she flipped through it and said sharply, "That's no good. My sister can make it up as good as that"—welcome evidence, at least, that the shop was not attracting only the converted.

With the first volume of Edward Marsh's *Georgian Poetry*, the Poetry Bookshop imprint at once became famous, and the shop was coping with a "sell-out" even before the official opening. The printers promised five hundred copies by December 1, 1912 to catch the Christmas market. Orders poured in, but the first batch of 250 copies was not ready until December 16. At Marsh's flat a team of packers, including Monro and del Re, with Rupert Brooke and Lascelles Abercrombie, worked late at night sending off review copies. By December 20 the book had sold out, and the second batch of copies did not arrive until Christmas Eve: a classic introduction to life as publisher and bookseller.

Georgian Poetry, the new paper *Poetry & Drama* and Ezra Pound's anthology *Des Imagistes*, published by Monro in 1914, made the shop widely known to those interested in poetry. It became a place of resort for students from the near-by University, who spent their lunch hours reading the new books; for young writers from the provinces, visitors from abroad, poets of all persuasions: Pound himself, red-bearded, green-eyed, didactic, with wide-open shirt collar and flowing black silk bow; Ralph Hodgson, a bluff north-countryman, with pipe and bull terriers, shying away from talk of poetry, but willing to chat about billiards or boxing; and those not yet in print, some of them bringing their verses along with them. One of the rejected, advised not to attempt publication just yet, swept out with a crushing retort—"Only the great can appreciate the great." Another, who lodged over a coffee-shop across the street, was impressed by Monro's criticisms and elated by his praise. He was Wilfred Owen.

Monro was generous with such help, and in the long run favourable to newer trends, though apt to be cautious or impatient in his first response. Richard Aldington, whose early Imagist work he published, said later that "Harold had been the Marshal Joffre of contemporary poetry— always ten minutes late and two divisions short"; a piece of flippancy which, writes Aldington, "was too true to be relished; and so I was disinherited." For later generations, brought up to revere the mournful love-notes of J. Alfred Prufrock and the delicate silverpoint landscapes of Edward Thomas—both at first declined by Monro—it is even more easy to deride such caution. But, as his own work shows, he was innately sympathetic to the new stylists and would find his own place among them: although in doing so he must have come to realise that his old dream of helping poetry in a new modern idiom to reach a wider public was in itself a paradox.

Hard-up poets and others were lodged at a nominal rent of 3/6 a week (often unpaid) in two attics above the Bookshop. Robert Frost, when some poems were accepted for *Poetry & Drama,* "took it out in room rent," finding Jacob Epstein, his wife and his current block of stone next door. Eric Gillett sold his stamp collection to pay for his attic when he came for a few weeks from Cheshire, and on the day that the first number of Percy Wyndham Lewis's *Blast* came out he saw Devonshire Street black with clergymen coming in to buy it: "word had got round that *Blast* was to be a very scurrilous publication." The lodgers added to the Bookshop legends and sometimes to Monro's problems; the Lawrences holding one of their famous quarrels at midnight, when Frieda hurled D.H. through a partition into the next room; and a woman visitor—who, like Hans Andersen, could not perch at that height without a fire-escape rope—having to be rescued when she lost her nerve during a daylight practice. No wonder some of them found their host's welcome on the gloomy side.

"The reading—not *recitation*—of poetry became a ceremony twice a week," writes Dr del Re. First in a small room upstairs, later in a converted goldbeating workshop at the back of the premises, or—for the most popular occasions—in a public hall near by, people crowded to hear de la Mare murmuring his poems in a dreamlike atmosphere, his face in shadow, green light from a shaded oil lamp falling across his book; W. H. Davies, rigid with stage fright beforehand despite "a large dose of whisky," but going on to give a splendid performance; Brooke, just back from the South Seas, "beautiful as an annunciating angel"; the actor Henry Ainley reading Hardy's poems; and the strange sing-song chanting of Yeats, who would stand with head thrown back, pince-nez perched precariously, a lock of black hair falling across his forehead. From 1915 onward the readings were held weekly, and among hundreds who read their own work were T. S. Eliot, Ford Madox Ford, Ezra Pound, Edith Sitwell, Anna Wickham.

A generous host, it was one of Monro's pleasures to bring together men of "like or unlike" mind and provide a fireside where they could talk half the night. Guest lists are frequent in his diaries; each looking, predictably, like an index of writers. For November 11, 1913 the list ran: Thomas, Davies, Flint, Hodgson, de la Mare, Plarr, Hewlett, Squire, Frost, del Re. Ten years later he was jotting down nearly fifty names within two days, among them Alec Waugh, Wolfe, Flint, the Sitwell brothers, Bax, Gould, Read, Shanks, Palmer, Moncrieff, Marsh, Eliot, Dukes, Nevinson, Ould, Dobrée. List-making was typical of his neat and methodical ways. Other lists record his personal expenses, poems written and fees earned, poetry readers and works to be read. An excellent organiser and careful business man, it was not his fault that the shop could not pay its way. Not surprisingly, with so much on his mind, he sometimes hankered after freedom and solitude. Like other writers, he needed seclusion and the sense of empty hours ahead to work; then lively and varied company in the reaction from writing. In many ways the busy life of the shop suited him. "Boredom," he noted early in 1913, "is the source of most evils"—and he can rarely have been bored in these crowded years of his life. In the day-to-day running of the place, however, he needed an active manager to relieve him from routine work. Almost at once he found this partner in Alida Klementaski, a beautiful girl of Polish descent whose idealism and devotion to poetry matched his own. She also had great vitality, shrewd practical ability, a sense of theatre and a lively talent for ridicule. Her business methods were at times informal—once, on going abroad, she wrote to warn her executor that she had left £500 hidden up a chimney and a further sum in banknotes in a book called *Alice-For-Short*—but all her life she had a flair for success in anything she undertook.

Their first encounter was promising. Young Miss Klementaski, at twenty, wanted to "reform the world," to be a doctor, to write, to go on the stage. Meanwhile, despising the antics then practised by the "elocutionist," she had trained herself to read verse simply and with genuine feeling. In March 1913 she was invited to read some of Monro's work at a poets' dining club. She was given a copy of *Before Dawn* and told to make her own choice. Borrowing "a terra-cotta velvet Liberty dress" from a sculptor friend, she set out on a stormy night to go by bus from Hampstead to the Monico: "It was terribly wet, and I was so wrought up that I dropped Harold Monro's book in the gutter when I got off the bus, and then muddied my wonderful velvet dress in picking it up." But the reading went well: "One of the poems I read was *Go Now, Beloved,* a very dramatic poem and horribly jealous: because Harold Monro was terribly jealous. Afterwards he spoke to me and thanked me, and said how surprised he was at having them read so well, because he had expected the usual elocutionist: but he wished I hadn't read *Go Now, Beloved.* But I said I liked it because it was so dramatic. Then he wrote in the copy, 'In memory of a perfect rendering, and of a grudge.' From that time we became friends. He found that I only lived for poetry and we often used to think what an extraordinary thing it was that we should have met. I was the ideal companion to be with him in running the Bookshop, and I started there in the autumn of 1913, after my father died. I knew reams of poetry by heart. I was able to read the work that was sent in, and for the rest of Harold's life I arranged the programmes for the readings. Of course I used to write verse. Harold always said that I had an extraordinary gift and lucidity. But he didn't encourage me, because one of us was enough. I absolutely adored him and all that I could do for him I did."

It was due to her that the Bookshop survived the war. Monro—having tried in vain to enlist at once—was called up in 1916, when he was 37, and sent to an anti-aircraft battery at Shoeburyness in the Thames estuary. There he saw two of the worst Zeppelin raids before going on to another anti-aircraft station near Manchester. The nervous strain of service life was too much for him, and after a breakdown he was transferred in 1918 to intelligence work at the War Office, which had its own trials for the conscientious: if the Germans did anything heroic, he told Alida Klementaski, instructions were that "essential but not literal" truth must be given.

In Devonshire Street, Alida was working almost single-handed, teaching herself book-keeping, lettering and design, keeping up the weekly readings and coping with the daily round: "Each morning I used to get the post ready, do up the day's orders, then go round the corner and get a little handbarrow which I used to push up to the carrier's in Goswell Road, dump my parcels, then go back to open up the shop. I often stayed there till 1 a.m. doing invoices. I used to colour our rhyme sheets by hand, and all the copies of Harold Monro's *Strange Meetings*, published in 1917, with Lovat Fraser's drawing on the cover. Ralph Hodgson had handed over the Flying Fame publications (poetry chapbooks and broadsides). John Nash did covers for Richard Aldington's *Images* and Flint's *Cadences*—a weeping willow for Aldington's, a swan for Flint's—and I used to colour them with coloured inks. Charlotte Mew (poet of *The Farmer's Bride*) would take a roll of rhyme sheets and go home to colour them. I designed the covers for some of the books, and the lettering—I had done the lettering for Harold's *Children Of Love* in 1914. I published and distributed *Georgian Poetry III* and *IV* entirely on my own. I never had a spare moment. I was just living for what I was doing."

At the end of the war, like many others, Monro was restless, looking forward to his release and longing to simplify his life. "I serve 7 masters," runs a cryptic note made in January 1919; "which service shall I resign?" It had been a triumph, in that first wave of enthusiasm, to make a success of the "slum Bookshop" and of publishing; but now Alida realised that he might never return to it. The war had given him little chance to think of his own poetry. New themes and new friends claimed him. He could have retired from drudgery and financial sacrifice, returning to the easy delightful life he had known before 1911. But he did not. He went back to found a new paper, *The Monthly Chapbook*, to replace *Poetry & Drama*, which the war had finished; and to face post-war setbacks of every kind, trade depression, strikes, illness and personal unhappiness. Even before he left the War Office in March 1919 he held a series of "stag parties" to bring together the survivors and the new poets.

Did people always appreciate his efforts on their behalf? Needless to say, they did not. "It was not his fault," wrote Flint, "that the irritable tribe did not respond as generously as he invited." E. H. W. Meyerstein used to assure him that "any sort of communistic idea in poetry is ridiculous. It is, barring music, the most individualistic of the arts." But there were some like Osbert Sitwell, who found him "the most considerate and, indeed, inspired of hosts"; and Douglas Goldring, who wrote years later: "I look back on those Poetry Bookshop gatherings with the warmest emotion of gratitude to Monro for having organised them. No one else in London at the time could possibly have collected together so many poets and writers under such friendly and informal conditions. I suppose I have been, in my life, to some hundreds if not thousands of literary parties, but I cannot recall any which I enjoyed as much and at which I made so many friends."

Funds were always low, and losses sometimes totalled as much as £500 a year—a large part of Monro's private income. During the later months of 1916, weekly takings varied from about £5 to £11 17s 6d. In the 1920s the readings, at an entry fee of sixpence, brought in only about £80 a year. In 1927, after the shop had removed to Great Russell Street, opposite the British Museum, Alida wrote: "Things are the slightest bit better here, but bank balance only £28. How we shall go on I do not know." As before, they went on by continual subsidies from Monro's own money.

The Bookshop—the first serious attempt in England to sell poetry—was the forerunner of poetry sections in all modern bookshops. By the time it closed in 1936, established poets knew that their books would be in stock elsewhere. For the young newcomer, hoping to launch his first slim volume and to meet other writers, nothing has ever taken its place. To go on with this work for the rest of his life called for all the steadfastness of character which Harold Monro shared with Alida.

Their long partnership had its shadowed side. It was always based on love and friendship; and after his divorce in 1916 she wrote to him tentatively about their future: "In idea yours, but not in practice: isn't that so?" Her account of their eventual marriage, on Easter Saturday 1920, gives a rather grim insight into the social pressures of fifty years ago: "Harold didn't believe in marriage and neither did I. I said I was perfectly prepared to live with him if he was prepared to tell everyone that we didn't agree with marriage; but it was awkward sometimes. Then McKnight Kauffer (the artist) told Harold he was doing a terrible thing and that it was wrong not to marry me. Finally we got married at the Register Office in Clerkenwell. Harold provided no ring, but I had a very charming antique cameo ring of my own. We had witnesses brought in from outside. It was an awful day to get married, there were crowds —we got over it, whizzing through, and I got my certificate. Harold tore off afterwards and I went to stay with a friend. Later I had a letter from Harold—a man had asked if he were married and he'd said 'No.' He was furious when people began congratulating him, and he didn't want his ex-wife even to see me."

They continued to make their homes apart, meeting at the Bookshop, where she was still known as Miss Klementaski, and at cottages they took in Sussex. But three years later she was writing sadly, in reply to some reproach about her devotion to her dogs: "It is absolutely necessary to one's happiness to have someone to care for the whole time—it might be children—or you. At one time I simply longed to have a house with you and look after all your physical and material needs and you wouldn't hear of it. I love you and give you all the love I can, but really you don't seem to need it. If I were of a different temperament I should fill my life with other friends and amusement. As it is I can't get to know other people, men especially, because I feel it is disloyal to you. It is the dogs that keep me for you, otherwise when I felt as lonely as I used without them I should turn elsewhere for the companionship I do not get in you." The letter goes on: "I assure you that alcohol is all the trouble. I can't tell you how I loathe the alcoholic state." In another letter she spoke of her deep sadness at seeing Nigel, his son by his first marriage, and remembering that they had no child.

About "the alcoholic state" she had come to know a great deal: that sombre choice, as one victim has said, "between drinking or being too depressed to go on; until in the end one is too ill to go on." His addiction became for her the Strange Companion of his early poem, and at the end of her life she admitted, "We had terrible times." But she would never allow Monro or herself to believe that he could not be cured. Her letters, written frequently when they were apart, contain advice that is often sensible—"The fact of taking alcohol continuously prevents you from eating enough food to keep your nerves in order. If you were to have a beefsteak every time you had that let-down feeling you would need alcohol less"—and sometimes touchingly optimistic: "Have you bought Yeast Vite? It may be of some use to you because it has the same action on the stomach as alcohol—which creates yeast ferment in the stomach."

To others she would behave as though alcoholism did not exist. "That was her way of dealing with the problem," writes a close friend of hers. "By remaining outside much of his life she maintained his great love, the Bookshop, the readings and publishing. She did him a great service in that way, and gave them a sense of achievement."

Both could rise to an occasion. As the unofficial representative of poetry, Monro was asked to lecture all over the country. The same friend remembers a literary function when he was so ill that his wife wrote his speech, rehearsed it with him in the taxi and sat beside him literally propping and prompting him through his piece. "Drama, drama keeps women going"; perhaps that was always true of Alida Monro.

Her sense of the dramatic could go with a spark of mockery. At one time she had in her possession a letter of T. S. Eliot's which she knew Eliot would wish destroyed. Her way of reassuring him was not to return the letter privately, but to produce it at a dinner party and, with an impressive word of explanation, burn it with her cigarette lighter under the eyes of the poet and fascinated guests.

For the readings, in which she often took part, and for other public appearances, she designed striking and unusual handmade dresses in keeping with the Bookshop "image" of beauty and simplicity. When her husband died she was thirty-nine, but barely half her life was over; and although she closed the shop four years later, feeling that it had had its day, she went on to use her gifts in other ways.

xxi

She flew to America five times, to lecture on modern poetry and the Bookshop, and also to judge at dog shows. At her Sussex country home she bred miniature poodles with great success, producing many champions, and their Kennel Club "prefix" name Firebrave—coined long before by Harold Monro—became world famous among dog owners. She remained devoted to poetry, acting as adjudicator at verse-speaking festivals, and was for some years the only woman on the board of judges at an annual festival of speech held at Oxford. Always a fearless and forthright critic, she was particularly intolerant of what she called, in a phrase later used by the telephone service, "the girl with the golden voice"—an echo of Dowson's *Girl With The Golden Eyes*—who showed no understanding of poetry.

Both Dr del Re and Flint thought Alida influenced the development of Monro's own work. "She had an incisive mind and a keen sense of the ridiculous," wrote Flint. "Before the laughter in her cool clear eyes, many of Harold Monro's phantasms and romantic illusions and much of his derivative speech must have vanished, never to return again." Because of their likeness of thought, she could at times unconsciously suggest a theme for a poem—*Real Property* is a response to a letter she wrote from Dorset in August 1916. *The Terrible Door* he dictated to her in coming round from an operation. But by the time they met he had probably passed through his early periods of imitation and experiment, and was already finding his own voice, stimulated by his success as a critic and by the company of other poets; although, as T. S. Eliot said, "Had Monro been a poet who could have worked out his own method in isolation, and ignored the attempts of his contemporaries, he might earlier have found a more personal idiom."

Seriousness is the keynote of his work. Like many Scots, his outlook on life was naturally grave, and he could not care for English humour and word play: a blind spot which sometimes betrays him into a vein of naivety from the reader's point of view. He was irritated by one eminent poet who could relax in company—"giggly" was Monro's damning epithet; and William Plomer records that he was not amused, after the appearance of *Milk For The Cat*, to be greeted with *Miaow, miaow*! "Monro turned, looked displeased, and said in a serious tone: 'That's a *good* poem, Z. That's a *good* poem.'" He was frankly puzzled by the inclusion of *Overheard On A Saltmarsh* and *Milk For The Cat* in school anthologies, demanding, "What is the teacher to say when a little girl asks, 'What's a *creeping lust?*'" One might suggest that, so vivid is the picture evoked, no child would ask such a question, except perhaps in the cause of entertainment; and in doing so one must see how right he was to be concerned, for such inclusion has often led to complete misjudgement of his quality. Entertainment was not his aim.

Monro was one of the first to protest at the attachment of the "soldier poet" label to Brooke; "as if," Christopher Hassall said later, "one should characterise Wordsworth by *The Happy Warrior*." For Monro himself to be characterised by these two gentle pieces, together with *Children Of Love*, is far more incongruous. These three, with other domestic and pastoral pieces, were the expression of hidden anguish; an attachment to familiar or childlike images in the face of growing desolation. As T. S. Eliot realised, one must read the whole of his work to see this: "The external world, as it appears in his poetry, is manifestly but the mirror of a darker world within. It takes the form sometimes of what a superficial glance might dismiss as the whimsical: talking Beds and Teapots"—a rather unkind hint from the poet of *Rhapsody On A Windy Night*, with its talkative street lamp.

"His difficulties in expression must have been consider-

xxiii

able," Eliot wrote. "He is at the same time very intimate and very reticent. He does not express the spirit of an age; he expresses the spirit of one man, but that so faithfully that his poetry will remain as one variety of the infinite number of possible expressions of tortured human consciousness.

"It takes time. There is no one poem, no few poems, which I could point to and say: this will give you the essence of Monro; the nearest approach, and the dourest excruciation, is his *Bitter Sanctuary*. This one poem must at least demonstrate that Monro's vision of life was different from that of any of his contemporaries."

Different; solitary; and often far ahead: in *Great City*, for instance:

> When I returned at sunset,
> The serving-maid was singing softly
> Under the dark stairs, and in the house
> Twilight had entered like a moonray . . .

and the companion piece, *London Interior*:

> Time must go
> Ticking slow, glooming slow.
>
> The evening will turn grey.
> It is sad in London after two . . .

How far is this twilit city from "the drowsy golden Georgian dream," and how near to the post-war mood of *The Waste Land*, published eight years later; just as Monro's salute to the outbreak of war, in *Retreat* and *Carrion* (1914), foreshadows the realism of Sassoon and Owen, and has little in common with poems about "the rich dead" or the humble city clerk "who goes to join the men of Agincourt." *Officers' Mess* (*1916*) might have been written by a poet of the second world war; and the unwary countryman of

xxiv

Strange Meetings—though seen through a townsman's eyes
—has a dire message in 1970:

> So they mistook him for a clod of land
> And round him, while he dreamed, they built a town.
> He rubs his eyes; he cannot understand,
> But like a captive wanders up and down.

In a lecture at Cambridge in 1912 Monro had defined the contemporary poet as "the poet that had caught the spirit of Darwin, that spirit which had so altered our attitude, and rendered obsolete so many ways of talking about life." Earlier, in 1908, his diary shows how profoundly he felt the loss of religious faith: "It is taking me nothing less than appalling time to get accustomed to the idea of no individual immortality. But now I begin to say: As it is true, I will not suffer so." But he never escaped from that suffering, and the nearer he brought himself to death, the greater became his dread: no discharge in that war. The time came when the bad dreams that always troubled him became the spectres of delirium tremens. One after another the solaces of friendship, of familiar scenes, even of wine, deserted him; only "the cup of sleep" remained. His own alternative title for *Bitter Sanctuary* was *The Alcoholics*.

Monro is like that unfortunate in a story by Dr M. R. James, who, pursued by monstrous apparitions called up by himself, vainly takes refuge in a peaceful lodging: "What can he do but lock his door and cry to God?" What is remarkable is that he has left such a clear record of that mental climate, in poetry that does not spare the reader, and gives him a vision he will find nowhere else: *A summons; an alarm; a drive; a call, A cry beyond an iron unopened door* . . .

To face life haunted by his own fate, and by the terrible indolence of the disillusioned, must have called every day for a fresh effort of will. What it cost him can be seen in the beautiful poem *Living*: one of those by which perhaps he is best remembered.

And yet it would be wrong to picture Monro's life as one of continual gloom and introspection. He himself saw the danger of this and tried to keep himself occupied. In London he lunched and dined almost daily with writers and artists, going on to concerts, lectures and plays; on January 21, 1929, to the memorable first night of *Journey's End*, presented by his old friend Maurice Browne. An evening alone was rare enough to be noted in his diary. In the country he enjoyed tennis and long walks, and he was often abroad.

He always showed great courage in overcoming illness. In 1927 came one of his worst ordeals, when he went almost blind; due, Mrs Monro thought, to nicotine poisoning when he was allowed to smoke after a sinus operation. He recovered his sight after a long course of treatment in Switzerland; but in 1931 his health again deteriorated. The next winter he was staying at Broadstairs while his wife travelled up and down between shop and nursing home. On March 14, 1932, his 53rd birthday, she realised that he was very ill, and as she left he told her, "I think this just about ends your day with me." He had asked for some writing-blocks for poems as a birthday present, and she went out to buy them; but a month before he had written his last poem:

> Oh, the dull mirror! Never will it hold
> A new reflection, less deformed and old?
> Roll up the long scroll, far too long unrolled.

She never again saw him conscious, and he died two days later.

The Times, in a long obituary article, praised all he had done for poetry, his rare devotion to the ideal of fraternity among poets, his steady capacity for improvement in his own work. A few poets found their way to his funeral; among them E. H. W. Meyerstein, who, with characteristic heart and bite, went home and wrote to a friend:

"This man helped dozens and dozens of people to get their names up (never me, I may say; you won't find me in any of his anthologies), he got them to give recitations, printed them and what not. Would you not have thought the crematorium would have been packed? Nobody did this but Monro—and when he dies, he is hardly followed to the grave.

"Of course I was secretly amused, as I always am now, by the frustration of human hopes. I have no illusions left on that score, or very few."

Monro might have said the same. He was never looking for gratitude; friendship he always valued, and the sense of creative achievement. To have written some poems he thought worth while, and to have his work accepted by T. S. Eliot and published in *The Criterion*, must have been a source of pride, even in his last illness.

A visitor to the Bookshop readings described how, when the hour struck, he would appear before the waiting crowd, draw aside the curtains at the back of the shop and, with a faint smile and "stiff little soldierly bows and a slight wave of the hand," invite them to enter. Each autumn he would open the new session by himself reading Shelley's *Hymn To Intellectual Beauty*:

Love, Hope and Self-esteem like clouds depart
And come, for some uncertain moments lent . . .

Since that poem first captured him he had travelled a long way, often in great bitterness of spirit; but he had these moments, and they were his reward.

CONTENTS

THE SICKROOM

A WRINKLED hag beyond the reach of gloom,
Whom even grief neglects, but on a tomb
She mumbles (which has now become this room)
    Her groping moan of pain.

Pain?—Can he be that wily ghost who creeps
From corner into corner?—Then he leaps
With pinch, thud, grip and yell; recoils and weeps
    Waiting to leap again.

Oh, the dull mirror! Never will it hold
A new reflection, less deformed and old?
Roll up the long scroll, far too long unrolled.
    Throw down the toppling stone.

People move out, move in, all far away.
Is there a difference between night and day?
In which direction move the hours? But, stay!
    Who groaned? Ah, me! Who groaned?

BITTER SANCTUARY

I

SHE lives in the porter's room; the plush is nicotined.
Clients have left their photos there to perish.
She watches through green shutters those who press
To reach unconsciousness.

I

She licks her varnished thin magenta lips,
She picks her foretooth with a finger nail,
She pokes her head out to greet new clients, or
To leave them (to what torture) waiting at the door.

II

Heat has locked the heavy earth,
Given strength to every sound,
He, where his life still holds him to the ground,
In anæsthesia, groaning for re-birth,
Leans at the door.
From out the house there comes the dullest flutter;
A lackey; and thin giggling from behind that shutter.

III

His lost eyes lean to find and read the number.
Follows his knuckled rap, and hesitating curse.
He cannot wake himself; he may not slumber;
While on the long white wall across the road
Drives the thin outline of a dwindling hearse.

IV

Now the door opens wide.

He: "Is there room inside?"
She: "Are you past the bounds of pain?"
He: "May my body lie in vain
    Among the dreams I cannot keep!"
She: "Let him drink the cup of sleep."

2

Thin arms and ghostly hands; faint sky-blue eyes;
Long drooping lashes, lids like full-blown moons,
Clinging to any brink of floating skies:
What hope is there? What fear?—Unless to wake and see
Lingering flesh, or cold eternity.

O yet some face, half living, brings
Far gaze to him and croons:
She: "You're white. You are alone.
    Can you not approach my sphere?"
He: "I'm changing into stone."
She: "Would I were! Would *I* were!"
Then the white attendants fill the cup.

VI

In the morning through the world,
Watch the flunkeys bring the coffee;
Watch the shepherds on the downs,
Lords and ladies at their toilet,
Farmers, merchants, frothing towns.

But look how he, unfortunate, now fumbles
Through unknown chambers, unheedful stumbles.
Can he evade the overshadowing night?
Are there not somewhere chinks of braided light?

VII

How do they leave who once are in those rooms?
Some may be found, they say, deeply asleep

In ruined tombs.
Some in white beds, with faces round them. Some
Wander the world, and never find a home.

ON THE DESTRUCTION OF THE FOUNDLING HOSPITAL

NOW at the last grave moment who will come?
The scheme is ready; architects have made
Their plans, they say.
And so, to-morrow, what has been to-day
A lovely home
For trees and birds and children will become
Piled up with cranes and girders and the numb
Loud hammer will resound, the concrete grow.—O, some
Lover of air and trees and ground, do move
In charitable love!

Let us not tell
Of those first traitors who
Sold Coram's heart. That bitter tale is well
Untold.
But listen, you, and you!
All that is needed, is to save, to save;
And now the chance grows every hour more cold.

Think of the future, when they not yet born
Will mourn: "Here was a lovely park, where trees
And children grew together. It was torn
—Corruptly—out of London to build these;
And children have no spaces left for play."

4

A traitor to Mankind is man to-day.
What can we do? What offer? How contrive
To keep those trees and all that ground alive?

THE ONE, FAITHFUL . . .

HOW many many words may pass
Before one ever makes a friend
And all that conversation prove, alas,
However subtle, nothing in the end.

Searching I found and thought, "I will enrol
You slowly, peacefully among those of mine
Who can pass out beyond the initial toll
Of comradeship through necessary wine."

But, probing, I discovered, with what pain,
Wine more essential in the end than you,
And boon-companionship left me again
Less than I had been, with no more to do
Than drop pale hands towards their hips and keep
Friendship for speculation or for sleep.

We persons multiplied upon this earth
Meet hardly ever, or when we have found
Each other built congenial by our birth
Then we, just then, suspect the common ground
The voice, the way, the manner and the sound.

Friendship may be too difficult to win—
May end too quickly in a faint distrust,

Or may be found too sharply to begin
In its mere finding, a disgust.

So shall I turn to you my only friend
And going to you find you always there?
(I thought that) I return to you. I bend
My lips towards your eyes for what I miss
But just as we are sloping toward our kiss
I feel them moistened by your lonely tear.

UNTO HER

O, FLOWER of my life, I bring my heart
To you, and find you waking with a start.

The bed is made, and you, half smile, half frown;
Have been a tedious two hours lying down.

Have dozed and wakened, dozed and waked again,
Imagined joy, felt everlasting pain.

I come, I come; I bring, I bring my grief,
That burns my dismal soul without relief.

But your slim arms receive me in their fold,
You warm my heart. My body that was cold

Receives your lifefull gift, and now I find
Peace and eventual Heaven in your mind;

And in your body, that one place I have sought,
A tranquil lodging for my stormy thought.

6

BLURRED ETCHING

INCREDIBLE. So near to paradise.
Time; Death: halt! Oh, what gardener has been here?
Are the trees conscious? Are they, even, wise?
Do they know Adam when he wanders near?
He touches them. They answer through the lake.
They love the wind that leans to comb their leaves.
(When a bird sings, then all its feathers shake.)
And yet when Adam thinks the garden grieves.
He should not give unconsciousness a name.
No sound. Low wind. Still water. . . . Then a man
Under the weeping willow roughly came,
And idly kicked an empty old tin can
Into the lake, but only to the fright
Of one lank swan who wanders, lonely, white.

NEW DAY

AND how will fancy lead his life to-day?
Eyes lift their shutters. Still the room is grey.
But slowly it reveals (with blankets back)
Omens all clothed in blue; or green; or black.
How will the small things of the day behave?
Will hope be calm, or petulantly rave?

There'll be no great decision. Time will knit,
And multiply the stitches while we look.
A few hours we shall stand, a few hours sit,
A few hours talk, or walk, or read a book.

7

The dishes will be washed, the table laid.
Smells of sweet food will spread delicious wings.
The daily commonplaces will be said,
And we shall handle all the daily things.

And so the time will pass.
Yet is there not a meaning in our looks
That makes us kindred as the blades of grass,
Or tree-leaves leaning over country brooks?
May we not be aware somehow
Among the cool small habits we have made
Of calm hands or a sympathetic brow,
Or of a guiding motive in the shade?

Yes ! Yes ! Oh what delusion have I had?—
Only to-day discovered you?
No wonder yesterday remained so sad.
Let us find out what Love intends to do.
Meanwhile for me
The moments will be only two or three.
Some little glance of yours will send me mad;
Some other look of yours will set me free;
Some word you drop make my whole body sad.
Some thing you do will send my spirit flying
Into the blue of wild delight;
And next the thought of you will leave my body lying
In passionate waking dreams all through to-night.

ELM ANGEL

O, WHY?—
Only a dove can venture that reply.

Large lawns were laid as far as eye could reach;
Ocean lolled inward on a cool long beach;
A tall town motionless and breathless gleamed;
The dead half-listened and their mind half-dreamed;
Wrecks trembled deep in their perpetual tomb;
A quiet drooped upon the summer room.
Now a blue hooded honeysuckle lane,
A garden built of roses on the wane,
Sahara buried under naked sand,
A boy with large eyes from an eastern land,
Muffled islands with hushed seas between
And one white temple glowing through the green;
Or, coming back, no place but only sound,
No elm that grew from any earthly ground,
But, heavenly throughout the atmosphere,
One ring dove cooing, crooning, cooing—Where?

COUNTRY RHYMES

COMPANIONS

OUR home in England must be filled with oak,
Carved in large form, and shining in the gloom.
From five to seven logs will light the room,
Where three or four companions talk and smoke,
Or dream, and wonder how the world began,
And why, and we will listen while you tell,
According to that tale you love so well,
Utopian happiness for final man.

The Walk

To-day the hills look dry and green.
The wind is cool, and we will walk.
Bring all the dogs. We shall have been
Ten miles, when, at the dusk, we come
Back to the honeysuckled home,
Where after supper some can doze, and some
By that red inglenook can think and talk.

Evening

Come to the ocean. Let us brave the wind
Along the plain. Oh, step by step, we hear
The rolling roar more clearly. Now how clear
Each separate wave. Pray, carry in your mind
That old refrain. For you will sit and think
This evening by the fire, or talk and drink;
And then you must repeat it in your head,
Before you sink
Into a doze sea-given, and we pass
(Laughing to hear you snore) another glass.

THE HURRIER

O FURROWED plaintive face,
No time for peace?
Indeed, keep your appointment.
Our great clock
Ticks in your spine, and locomotion wags
An angry tail.
Let toiling trailing tramway drive the point.
Hurry, or you are lost.—Everywhere

Hunger may lurk and leer.
You may have been elected among so many
To be his prey.
With horned imagination, drive your limbs.
O, it will need your whole life to be at peace.
Too many bland appointments intervene.
You have no time for death
And yet no time to hold your living breath.

THE WINTER SOLSTICE

WHILE they, those primitive men,
Were sacrificing all their fruits away,
Nevertheless the sun
Smouldered, and earlier sank each icy day,
Until at last his rays were so curtailed,
And they were driven back so far in dark,
That all began to think he might have failed.

In air they raised their gnarled and muscled arms,
Laying upon the troubled plain
Gigantic shadows, shrieking their alarms,
Invoking him, that only he remain,
Though, all the while, that old and regular sun
Gleamed on their frightened face,
Nor changed the purpose he had well begun.

At length when they discovered he was true,
That tortured season where he seems to go
Drowsing himself away in lemon blue
Under the earth, so low,

Became, no more a bleak lament for him,
But a large feast to glorify the rite,
The clean recapture of his former light.

We learned to flock together from the cold,
And mingle in the glow
Of rooms in which his captured gold
Provides ecstatic overflow . . .
While (memory can guess) plain-dutied Earth
Outside, and in the dark,
Is thrusting clumsy sap through stubborn clay,
And nearly, could one hark
Their crackling talk, one might discern the birth
Of leaves, and daffodils, and such as they.

LIVING

SLOW bleak awakening from the morning dream
Brings me in contact with the sudden day.
I am alive—this I.
I let my fingers move along my body.
Realisation warns them, and my nerves
Prepare their rapid messages and signals.
While Memory begins recording, coding,
Repeating; all the time Imagination
Mutters: You'll only die.

Here's a new day. O Pendulum move slowly!
My usual clothes are waiting on their peg.
I am alive—this I.
And in a moment Habit, like a crane,

12

Will bow its neck and dip its pulleyed cable,
Gathering me, my body, and our garment,
And swing me forth, oblivious of my question,
Into the daylight—why?

I think of all the others who awaken,
And wonder if they go to meet the morning
More valiantly than I;
Nor asking of this Day they will be living:
What have I done that I should be alive?
O, can I not forget that I am living?
How shall I reconcile the two conditions:
Living, and yet—to die?

Between the curtains the autumnal sunlight
With lean and yellow finger points me out;
The clock moans: Why? Why? Why?
But suddenly, as if without a reason,
Heart, Brain and Body, and Imagination
All gather in tumultuous joy together,
Running like children down the path of morning
To fields where they can play without a quarrel:
A country I'd forgotten, but remember,
And welcome with a cry.

O cool glad pasture; living tree, tall corn,
Great cliff, or languid sloping sand, cold sea,
Waves; rivers curving: you, eternal flowers,
Give me content, while I can think of you:
Give me your living breath!
Back to your rampart, Death.

SILENCE BETWEEN

Does not my ghost appear?
My eyes feel over intervening space,
  And I am leaning forward at the strain
Till, now, my fingers nearly touch your face.
  Lean out to me: I'm calling with my brain.

Do you not feel me near?
I'm bending forward on the wind of thought,
  Sailing toward you on the lake of mind.
O share this moment which may not be brought
  Ever to life again, once left behind.

But I can only hear
Far off the beating of your lonely heart,
  While in between us flow the hurrying waves.
A deathly wind is blowing us apart:
  Lovers are not more foreign in their graves.

GREAT DISTANCE

How can you be so far away?
When I have been in pain before
I've found you standing just outside
My body's door,
In patient silence waiting there,
That I might feel your spirit near.

But now, with every breath I take,
It seems that you have farther gone,

And I become more wide awake,
And more alone.
In all this world there is no light;
No open doorway here to-night.

I lay my body on the bed,
And cross my arms, and think of death,
And think, nine hundred miles away,
You draw calm breath.
At last, imagination through
That distance reaches out to you.

Now you are leaning on your hand,
And staring at an empty book.
You raise your eyes; you understand:
I feel your look
Pierce through me. In this foreign place
You reach me, and I know your face.

I swear that then our hands did touch,
And all my fainting pain is gone;
I know that you did touch my hand.
Each is alone.
Yet loneliness begins to seem
Like sleep, and will become a dream.

WHERE SHE LIVES

WE love the room; and it is ours;
But when I came to you to-day,
You were possessed by other powers:
You spoke, but you were far away.

I saw you pale against the wall,
Half hidden in a shaft of light.
I thought I heard a petal fall,
Yet disbelieved both sound and sight.

The traffic on the street roared by:
I trembled in the room alone.
I heard you move, then heard you sigh;
Yet wondered: Is she here, or gone?

Your lips were moved, yet, one by one,
Your words like dropping petals fell.
I whispered: surely, she is gone;
Cried inwardly: I cannot tell.

Room, come to life! Shine phantom wall!
Light, light, become you calm, and keen!
The shadows tremble, and are tall,
And everything is dimly seen.

Put your cold hands, and may they fall,
Loose, gently, on my tortured mind.
Room, come to life: shine phantom wall.

MIDNIGHT LAMENTATION

WHEN you and I go down
Breathless and cold,
Our faces both worn back
To earthly mould,
How lonely we shall be!
What shall we do,

You without me,
I without you?

I cannot bear the thought
You, first, may die,
Nor of how you will weep,
Should I.
We are too.much alone;
What can we do
To make our bodies one:
You, me; I, you?

We are most nearly born
Of one same kind;
We have the same delight,
The same true mind.
Must we then part, we part;
Is there no way
To keep a beating heart,
And light of day?

I could now rise and run
Through street on street
To where you are breathing—you,
That we might meet,
And that your living voice
Might sound above
Fear, and we two rejoice
Within our love.

How frail the body is,
And we are made
As only in decay
To lean and fade.

I think too much of death;
There is a gloom
When I can't hear your breath
Calm in some room.

O, but how suddenly
Either may droop;
Countenance be so white,
Body stoop.
Then there may be a place
Where fading flowers
Drop on a lifeless face
Through weeping hours.

Is then nothing safe?
Can we not find
Some everlasting life
In our one mind?
I feel it like disgrace
Only to understand
Your spirit through your word,
Or by your hand.

I cannot find a way
Through love and through;
I cannot reach beyond
Body, to you.
When you or I must go
Down evermore,
There'll be no more to say
—But a locked door.

THE OCEAN IN LONDON

IN London while I slowly wake
At morning I'm amazed to hear
The ocean, seventy miles away,
Below my window roaring, near.

When first I know that heavy sound
I keep my eyelids closely down,
And sniff the brine, and hold all thought
Reined back outside the walls of town.

So I can hardly well believe
That those tremendous billows are
Of iron and steel and wood and glass:
Van, lorry, and gigantic car.

SLEEPING BY THE SEA

THE tall old waves seethe onward to the beach,
With dismal loud explosion boom and fall
(Their reckless parent wind that follows each
Now nourishes them high, now starves them small).
They range like warriors battering a wall,
Who flood, invincible, gigantic, slow
Until their rising tide at length will reach
Their shattered town's indubitable fall.

But they are only furrows on the sea.
I, anxious bedded listener, stare and ask.
The generations climb Eternity;

The waves devour the shore: each wears a mask,
And each complacently fulfils a task.

The waves burst their cracked water. Their long blow
Furrows my anxious brain as I lie here.
They seem to drench me with their overflow;
But we are brothers, for we are so near
That I might well ignore them: yet I fear.
Their threat becomes terrific through their sound,
I shrink to earth; I burrow into ground.

TOO NEAR THE SEA

N̄O foam;
A trippling shallow tread;
The pebbles tingle on the beach,
While, disentangled over head
From clouds, the moonlight, carefully spread,
Lays whiter sheets on my white bed.

From haunted sleeplessness, in quivering dread,
I wander through the sea-sound-empty-full
Large sleeping room above that sea. My bed
Felt like a raft; but now there is the pull
Of dreary sea, toward the window drawing,
Of every slight wave with its itch and drag
Upward toward the tall lean windows clawing,
And, sea-bemysteried, my senses flag.
Yesterday and to-morrow will be waves
Breaking in calm succession on to-day.
Earth-life pales down to sea-foam. Flesh behaves

Like sifted ashes.
Cold slow ocean washes
All round, and then it washes me away.

THE GUEST

TALL, cool and gentle, you are here
To turn the water into wine.
Now, at the ebbing of the year,
Be you the sun we need to shine.

It is the birthday of your word;
And we are gathered. Will you come?
Let not your spirit be a sword,
O luminous delightful lord.

ROMANTIC FOOL

Romantic fool who cannot speak!

You are distant like a white cold cloud.
You pasture on the April sky.

I meet you with my head half bowed,
And wonder if you wonder why.
There has not been a single day
My eyes have dared look straight your way,
Or mix themselves with yours in play.

21

Your beauty fills my flesh with fear:
I flinch, as I have always done,
When loveliness became too near.
You dazzle me with your bright sun.
Supposing I should say a word
Just whispered lowly, as a bird,
While passing, and you smiled—and heard.

O then I fear that I might spring,
Utter some unearthly cry,
But drop my clipped and awkward wing,
Dumb, while you stared, and slowly I
Should have to pass your beauty by,

Becoming, like that bird, I think,
Beady-small, but vision-clear—
The epochs in between a sleep
Devoted to your being near,
Though your known face between my dreams
Is absent always, as it seems,
And I remain through week and week
Romantic fool who cannot speak.

JOURNEY TO RECLAIM A GHOST

NOW coming to the street where you had lived,
I trembled in cold fear.
Is it your ghost at that far corner?
Often you will have walked along this pavement.
I think you are not here.

O melancholy houses, ugly, grimy, small,
Two, two and two,
How are you changed! What glory did now fall
This moment over you!

I hesitated, nearly walked away.
Oh can it be the street?
What shall I do if I am doomed to meet
Your ghost to-day?

Suddenly all fearfulness has left me.
Gently I touch the knocker, quickly answered.
Inside the door, the hall,
There are they all:
Your mother and your sisters. No; not you.

We talk; we talk; until your ghost is here,
Enveloping our hearts; on mine too near,
For I had not intended to reply
To your loud knock.
They show your letters. Now what shall I do?
So curious and so keen have I become
Remembering you, and being in your home,
And realizing them and how they love
You, you. I cannot speak or move.
In their small parlour you are found and lost
You terrifying ghost.

How to be gone? How with no awkward stress
To leave you unto them, whom they possess?
Break through the atmosphere, the room,
The hall,
The door, the street and leave them all,
To me like ghosts themselves, in incandescent gloom?

What journey it has been to find your street!
Outside your street again, what shall I do?
Who are you really I have longed to meet?
What atmosphere have I disturbed?
Where may I wait,
Where watch the consequence
Of this adventurous trail of fate,
Or passionate chance?
What do?
Where journey hence
Away from you?

RUMOUR

SOMEBODY is whispering on the stair.
What are those words half spoken, half drawn back?
Whence are those muffled words, some red, some black?
Who is whispering? Who is there?

Somebody is sneaking up the stair,
His feet approaching every doorway,
Yet never a moment standing anywhere.

Now many whisper close outside some door.
O suddenly push it open wide.
You see: whoever said he heard them, he has lied.

And yet words are left dark like heavy dust
In many rooms, or red on iron like rust:
And who contrives to leave them? Some one must.

In every street, this noisy town of ours
Has stealthy whispering watchers walking round,

Recording all our movements, every sound,
Hissing and shuffling, and they may have found
To-day my name: to-morrow they'll find yours.

THE DARK STAIRCASE
(*A Fragment*)

WHEEL within wheel, mystery within mystery.
Yet we continue our gaunt uncanny pathway,
We three who thought each other one time faithful;
Hysterical, hypochondriacal,
Wordful as only the twentieth century can be,
Swearing under the shadowiness of alcohol
Loud oaths of loyalty never to be kept.

How ever did this argument begin?
I would that I had written it in a diary.
How did we lift this roof upon our heads?

How long shall I remain the gloomy victim
Of quibbles circumambulated round,
Promises exhausted on the lips,
Half-deeds without words, words without any deeds,
Threats and deluding changes of the voice,
Everlasting endless confabulation,
And no true foresight of what the end may not be:
Giving of hand without the feel of heart?

Evening on evening, night along to morning,
Our three hot souls return to argument,
Tormenting each other: weary have I become.

At length cannot you both be a little sorry?
Then, then only, kinship might prosper between us.

Often, when we have been in that room together,
I, returning at length to my own far house
And wondering inwardly, helplessly, inwardly,
Have, in a deep dark microscopic distance,
(And in my mental vision glued myself to them),
Beheld three people against a lonely background,
The unified reflections of ourselves,
Yet not ourselves. Oh now what are they doing,
Meeting and parting on a turret stair?
One at the top, one at the bottom, one
Or halfway up or halfway down, between them,
Carrying breathless messages to and fro?

And which of us can be which, and how did I,
Or carnally, or psychologically
Embroiled (I know not which) or when become
A unit in this trio? Are we playing
To some huge audience; or are we alone,
Without spectator, unimaginably. . . ?

THE TERRIBLE DOOR

TOO long outside your door I have shivered.
You open it? I will not stay.
I'm haunted by your ashen beauty.
Take back your hand. I have gone away.

Don't talk, but move to that near corner.
I loathe the long cold shadow here.
We will stand a moment in the lamplight,
Until I watch you hard and near.

Happy release! Good-bye for ever!
Here at the corner we say good-bye.
But if you want me, if you do need me,
Who waits, at the terrible door, but I?

STREET FIGHT

FROM prehistoric distance, beyond clocks,
Fear radiates to life
And thrills into the elbows of two men.
Fear drives imagination to renew
Their prehistoric interrupted throttle.

The street turns out and runs about,
And windows rise, and women scream;
Their husbands grunt, or scratch and hunt
Their heads, but cannot trace the dream.

Meanwhile those:
They rush; they close:
flick, flap, bang, bang, blood, sweat, stars, moon,
push, roar, rush, hold, part, bang, grind, swoon,
O slow, O swift, O now—But soon,

How soon the heavy policeman rolls in sight,
And barges slowly through that little crowd,
And lays his large hands calmly on those shoulders.
Now all will be exactly as it should be,
And everybody quietly go to bed.

Occasional spectator,
Do not you think it was very entertaining?

27

You, standing behind your vast round belly,
With your truss, your operation scar,
Your hairless head, your horn-rimmed eyes,
Your varicose veins,
Neuritis, neurasthenia, rheumatism,
Flat-foot walking, awkward straining of sinews,
Over the whole of your body
The slowly advancing pains of approaching death,
What comes into your mind when two men fight?

HOLY MATRIMONY

I

IT was a fatal trick to play upon him.
With lusty life all pointing to one aim,
And his whole body watchful:
She at the moment came.

Could he resist? Could she? That one blue glance
Was not her own: oh, a far stronger power
Than hers shone at him through her
And fixed their mating hour.

II

Words, hardly needed, then were spoken,
All having only one intent.
They walked like children staring downward,
With body toward body bent.

Now all the others mumble darkly,
Wonder and enviously stare.
There is a glowing in the household:
Desire will dwell a moment here.

But older eyes gleam coldly on them;
Stiffer bodies step between.
Now while the preparations start
They must be cleanly kept apart:
So has the custom always been.

"You cannot kneel before the altar
Until we've trimmed the lamp for you.
Meanwhile you may a little woo;
We've much to do:
We'll bake and sew and watch you sidelong,
And make your wedding bed for you."

III

But he and she
They hear, they stare,
And they are asking:
Who are we?

They cling and cry:
What have we done?
Through us what ceremonial
Is begun?

The dark doors close
Upon the sky.
They shall be locked within
Till they do die.

IV

O prison church! O warder-priest!
Now they who used to walk the wind of freedom
Are living in your gloomy house of stone;

And they and it are growing older;
She is becoming every day less fair.
The more together, they are more alone:
They pile the fire and yet the hearth is colder.

NATURAL HISTORY

THE vixen woman,
Long gone away,
Came to haunt me
Yesterday.

I sit and faint
Through year on year.
Was it yesterday
I thought her dear?

Is hate then love?
Can love be hate?
Can they both rule
In equal state?

Young, young she was,
And young was I.
We cried: Love! Come!
Love heard our cry.

Her whom I loved
I loathe to-day:
The vixen woman
Who came my way.

What was the time?
Which was the street
In which I thought you
Tame and sweet?

Now that again
I see your eyes
I do forget
I have grown wise.

Your argument
Has claim and poise,
But there's a vixen
In your voice.

Nightmare! O hard
To understand!—
She tried to give me
Her bright hand.

I sit and faint
Through year on year.
Was it yesterday
I thought her dear?

THE EMPTY HOUSE

WE were not wrong, believing that it cared;
When we had watched it gradually bared
Of furniture, I, going back alone,
Heard all its rafters moan.

It had become accustomed to our tread,
Our voices even, and the life we led.
I would wonder when I woke at night to hear
Its heart beating mysteriously near.

Or, when, arriving through the empty hall,
And feeling for the light, to catch the fall
Of shadows, where the ghostly rabble flies,
Frightened by human eyes.

(Ghosts are like instincts, little occupied
With time, and free of knowledge where they died.
They haunt, not having found the force to go,
Old houses they may know.)

Was it the mean desertion of a friend?
For all the time we plotted for the move
I thought the old house hearing: in the end
We nearly could not go because of love.

Toward the summer evening yesterday
What could I do but wander out that way?
And, looking at the house, what should I see,
From my own window staring back at me,

But my own image, definite and cold,
An early ghost, terrifyingly bold,
Haunting my former life, and making seem
My present body no more than a dream.

From that first moment many years ago
When first it did receive us, we by slow
Intent and movement modified the line
Of its design

So to receive our character and be
Friend to our various personality,
Gradually so to take us and to hold
Our furniture and form our outer mould,

That every angle slightly gave its place,
And even corners made a little space,
And open walls took shadow. But we are gone,
Except that I do haunt it still alone.

Unendingly imagination pries
Through every chink; the hand of memory tries
All darkened doors; the voice of habit falls
Along the empty walls.

And the strange dream lives on of those dead men
Who builded it together bit by bit,
And the forgotten people who since then
Were born in it, or lived and died in it.

GOD OF THE WORLD

I

IN the beginning there were raging voices,
Fierce cries of all the gods in tumultuous rivalry,
Pitting and girding the nations; limited though
And trimmed, and only a portion of the earth
Was bitten by the cruel fire of rival godhead.
That roar still rings through the world as an echoing echo.
Their large names yet do roll on the tongues of men.
For, each to each, "Here is my chosen people"

Thundered, and every little horde of humanity,
Having created its god, blinked and obeyed him.

That dwindled thunder reaches deafened ears.
We quiver but we will not lose our bearing.
Still the dust of their war blows into our eyes;
And the frightened hordes lift unexpected wails.
For even to-day old Zeus, ruined among his marble,
Or an older god, new named, might thunder upon Jehovah,
Though wheezy they would sound and pale would be their
    voices:
They would not quarrel like gods; their lightning would
    crackle damply.
But most of them are ghosts, or now they slumber
Deep in house of dust, or there are some who doze
In their own homesteads by their ancient fires
(Although they like and listen to their worship)
Nor dream of conquest nor of large possession,
Nor bargain through their envoys, nor send forth
Sombre missions, armed, nor covet heathen lands.
These dwell among their people—only not Jehovah.

II

Where dwell you now, Jehovah, many fabled,
Lord of the burning bush and of the mountain,
Explorer of the desert in your ark,
Devourer of your first-born, unbeloved?
You did not long endure your promised land,
Huge patriarch, but prepared a heavenly town,
A new Jerusalem, a celestial city.

It pleased you that your prophets should moan for you
On earth; your kings and judges and popes should rule

Vicariously, while you reclined in heaven.
O ancient Covenanter, bargain maker,
You will not claim to be father of Jesus?
Was it then you who feared that valiant angel
Satan, and drove him in disgrace from heaven?
By what gate does that wrinkled Peter snooze?
Your heavenly town, it may have many mansions:
What suburb has it large enough for Booth?
Or if you ever reigned there, did you leave
When General Booth arrived? Are you now on earth
Trying to reconcile your worldly kingdom,
(O Rock of Ages, O mighty Lord of War)
A bearded Semite heavily bejewelled,
Bemotored and beyachted and bemansioned?
It may be that you travel from continent
To continent, promoting your great wars,
On your little world,
Your revolutions and your market movements,
Inhabiting a hundred millionaires,
A thousand dediamonded matronly bosomed concubines;
War lords are your archangels, O Jehovah,
Or do you only hairdress; organgrind; beg?

But (if you ever reigned in heaven) there
The trumpets slowly fall, the pavements crack,
Your throne tilts over; now the Seraphim
Turn grey and listless; all the wings are furled,
And one by one sweet angels, unemployed,
Have innocently fallen fast asleep.

DREAM EXHIBITION OF A FINAL WORLD

I

THE murky curtains roll apart. A gigantic Proscenium.
Dawn.
The purple lips of the Siren begin to twitch.
Eastward, a giant arc-light reflects through my dream
Glaringly, into a forest of chimneys.
Heavy upon my chest the large gorilla squats,
Holding, loosely, my throat.

The pulley-sinewed God of Earth whose arm is like a
crane
Now will lever the cable to open the lip of the Siren.
She mutters; her great head is wobbling:
Then her cry
Rattles her throat, before rising through pouted mouth
To a whistle, a warble, a wild full blast and a shriek;
Now a screech as her cheeks puff out; and it gashes the
light.
Her hair in the wind of her howl is frayed on the sky.

Early dreaming-time has guttered away.
She dwindles. Her lips, her eyes are closing.
The light of morning hangs in ribbons, bulging.
Now the charabancs marshalled in regiments with hooter
roaring
Thunder around the earth, round the Great Exhibition.
Aeroplanes flood the sky writing the news, and heaven
Films to the world, and winks. Within the electric pro-
scenium
There shall be dawn every day, imitated;
Whatever the season, beautiful, artificial,
Such as the Worker loves, bright like a picture postcard.

The exhibition was planned to endure through final
    humanity.
(Hefty gorilla, lift your claws from my throat,
Lurking ancestor phantom of final world,
Pranked in a purple Top-hat.)

II

The Gate is rare and precious,
Built of granite, the last to be quarried on earth,
Guarded by armies of negroes pranked in helmets of scarlet.
Not far within are kept, in golden cages,
Small broods, diminishing, of those old beasts:
Last lion of earth, last tiger, rhinoceros, buffalo;
In marble tank the last large whale of ocean.
Honoured: each has a lecturer talking
Glibly of habit and haunt, day and night, day and night.
Here is a tiny forest, reared by an old-world expert,
Fanned, that it whisper well, by regulated zephyrs;
Near to which in a cage on wheels, lined with satin and
    moss,
To be moved at his mood, and filled with mechanical birds,
There lives, walking up and down, in tweed, with a stick of
    rarest ash-plant,
Murmuring, making a note, or sipping beer from a tankard,
(Gloated upon by the crowd),
Rarer than lion, or granite, the last, last, Nature Poet.

Beyond is the last great valley (Charabanc, Charabanc,
    roaring!)
Here are the old cascades,
Warranted still in their ancient courses,
Guaranteed to be haunted yet by the spirit of.beauty,

37

Mumbling mysteriously far within their barb-wire encircled
    enclosures;
And every train-and-villa-girdled mountain
Is crowned with proud hotels.

There stands the last cathedral. Out beyond,
The free and vast asylum of beliefs
(Encooped are they in one gigantic cold enclosure)
Folds all the faithful. They may build therein
Church, Meeting House, Synagogue, Mosque, or Chapel.
Dreamy cranes are waiting without to lift within that arid
    space,
Complete, ready for use, direct from the factory,
Chapel, church, or cathedral, of corrugated iron.
Under the pulpit where preaches the Pope Himself
Latest American upstart may roar; here Salvation Army
Mass bands. Here rules, at length, the Spirit of Freedom.
For nobody fights any more about any religion.
Nobody troubles the clock-work heart of the God,
Lest cog, chain, piston, crank of the great machine
Should waver to hear or argue, or break, like a heart.

III

But, oh! the Mob is roaring! Here is mob roaring!
Armies (here it is different), armies, howling revenge.
The narrow, enormous arena where rules the downturned
    thumb.
Charabanc massed. Epsom. Telescope, Nero! Nero!
Tank! Bomb! Tank! Bomb! Every Terminus ending here!
Beautiful hail of blood. Millions killed in a minute.
War final, War! Never a shortage of bodies.
Watch the game, heroes! Hurrying clouds of corpses!
(Only a Magnate need gnash his teeth at Another.)

"Card of the War, sir? No seats left.
One in the upper circle. Only a thousand guineas."
Here is the final Circus, here is the final . . .

IV

Gorilla clutching my heart!
Shall I waken at all from the last Exhibition?
Will there be forest again, and sunrise and cornfield, this
      morning,
Farmhouse, haystack, flowers in the garden,
Protective, patient tree, that leans over the roof,
Near the trembling dimpering sea, where the long sand is
      hot,
And the slow tide rises and falls.
Breezes play lightly through meadows in long, dwindling,
      sunsets.
You bathe your limbs, you talk slowly; birds are all friendly?

V

Nightmare of future earth, again must I try
To build you. How can you be vaguely constructed,
Torment of dream,
Threatening to conquer: what are you like?
Shall it be thus? Two battleships for feet,
Two Eiffel Towers for legs, for your thin arms,
Two cranes that, either, lift ten thousand tons;
Your ribs long spans of bridges, your cold heart
Big Ben; your liver, clogged with bile, your guts, infirm,
Cluttered with refuse; your large belching stomach
Bulging with factories you have gulpingly swallowed;
All regulated by your clockwork heart?

But when at last I come to try your face,
I can see nothing, though your purple Siren
(So, Dream) can stroke it with arthritic hand.

You are held together by millions of wires and cables.
Could I alone cut one, one, the whole would fall apart.

VI

Now the moment is here to throw the gaunt gorilla
(Clutching my heart and making my dream)
Shivering with apish calls across the room.
He tumbles along the wainscot, becomes a shadow
Made by my lord, the Sun, the real
Redeemer, transmitter, transfuser, creator, giver, Receiver.

I rise at the open window; see real trees,
Real fields, real men, real dogs, real—Oh, the Charabanc,
Real; and there's the new, tall, factory chimney,
Real: and there, his cart-load real with bricks
The sawdust jerry-builder trolleys along the road,
Real. And how shall I finally murder the vaunting gorilla?
How can I ever succeed in protecting life, life, from the
    dream?

THE EARTH FOR SALE

I

HOW perilous life will become on earth
When the great breed of man has covered all.
The world, that was too large, will be too small.

40

Deserts and mountains will have been explored,
Valleys swarmed through; and our prolific breed,
Exceeding death ten million times by birth,
Will halt (bewildered, bored),
And then may droop and dwindle like an autumn weed.

How shall we meet that moment when we know
There is no room to grow;
We, conscious, and with lonely startled eyes
Glaring upon ourselves, and with no Lord
To pray to: judged, without appeal,
What shall we feel?
He, being withdrawn, no supplicating cries
Will call Him back. He'll speak no farther word.

Can special vision be required to see
What few pale centuries will take us there,
Where, at the barrier of the future, we
Shall stand condemned, in serried ranks, and stare
At Nothing—fearing Something may appear?

The Earth is covered with large auction boards,
And all her lands are reckoned up for sale.
The spaces that are now called virgin soil
Will soon be bought, and covered with great breed
Of human seed;
And, when the driven hordes
Cry "Food!"—but find no more for any toil,
Fear, fear will strike all eyes and faces pale.
Then no one more will speak,
But, rising from a murmur to a wail,
One voice, for all, will, like a Siren, shriek.

Is there no pledge to make at once with Earth
While yet we have not murdered all her trees;
Before it is too late for oath or pledge;
While yet man may be happy in his birth—
Before we have to fall upon our knees,
Clinging for safety to her farthest edge?

It is not very noble that we kill
Her lions and tigers, all. Is that our reign?—
Then let us build ourselves on earth again.
What is the human will?

Is it so clearly better than the ant's?
And is our life more holy than the plants'?
They do fulfil their purpose every year,
And bring no pain, nor fear.

III

Woe to that miserable last mankind;
And, when I think of that, I have a dread
I may awake on earth, again, to find
Myself, among it, living, oh, not dead.

IV

I had been thinking of that final Earth.
Then I remembered she herself would lick
Her own lithe body clean, and from her girth
Wipe any vermin that might cling too thick.

Damned! Damned! Apparent conqueror to-day—
Oh, evanescent sway!
O drunken lust!
O swarming dust!

Man makes himself believe he has a claim
To plant bright flags on every hill he swarms;
But in the end, and in his own wild name,
And for the better prospect of his fame,
Whether it be a person or a race,
Earth, with a smiling face,
Will hold and smother him in her large arms.

UNANSWERED QUESTION

SHALL you and I leave everything behind,
Go westward walking,
Never again be conscious of the mind,
But walking, talking
Of flowers and birds and clouds, with no routine,
Not wonder ever again what consciousness may mean?

Shall you and I go eastward in grave thought
And inward prying,
Be conscious, introspective, haggard, caught
Sighing and whying;
With all clear mind and valuable breath
Expended on cold doubts about eventual death?

Will you and I, submitting to the wind,
Go northward roaring?

That may be one good way to leave behind
The too trim harbour mooring:
Partake some great campaign, some large experience, some
Worthy extensive excuse for returning glorious home.

Can you and I go southward without blame
Into the region we love,
Fading without desire for famous name,
Or calculated move?
Can we in sunlight, both contentedly,
Live without ambition, gazing at blue sea?

THE CURATE'S CHRISTMAS EVE

THE Curate and the Spinster sit.
  (O gentle drear timidity!)
Her yearning thought, his untried wit,
  Her aspidistra and their tea
Combine to make their Christmas Eve complete
Within itself; and neither sour nor sweet.

Why should the moralist complain?
  The sentimentalist deride?
She turns fond eyes on him in vain:
  She will not ever be a bride,
For he is doomed to pass eternity
Sipping, O, nothing more than, sipping tea.

She will not be compelled to scold,
  Nor he be driven to complain.
They are better both than any gold.

No mistletoe, and no champagne,
Will make her less a maid, him more a priest,
Or turn their Christian to a pagan feast.

IN THE NIGHT

OVER my head
The hard cool face of grief stares all the night.
My hateful bed
Is never silent, creaking every time I move.
I am tortured, fevered with the poison of love
All crumpled waiting for my love's delight.

The stupid hours die and then live again
Winding their cogged and ticking flight of pain.
Morning will come at last I fear, I know.
Strike the foul vengeful gong when I must rise
Patiently, quickly through the tired day go,
Curse my dear love and swallow its loud cries.

Where is your face you torturer, what are your hands
Doing so far away from eager mine?
I hope you may be sad in other lands
Tired, cold and suffering. Then my body flies
Voyaging to comfort you and intertwine
Its longing with your fate and with your sighs.

But are you dead? Then I become a ghost
Hovering and haunting like a bird of prey
Crying above you, I will dare the boast

I could pick out your soul and soar away
Into the night and bring you—you shall lie
In vain dead. I still love though you may die.

The face of grief floats through the haunted room
And covers all the furniture. Hard time
Will you not crack and flood about the gloom?
O, I am tired of this abortive rime
It does not bring you back friend far away—
Light claws between the curtains.—It is day.

LOVERS IN A LONDON SHADOW

Y OU two, who woo, take record of to-night;
(This corner, that arc-light):
For you may never feel again
Such joyful pain.

Your bodies, which do tremble, thrill and rock
In one bright carnal shock,
Will cool: your senses will relax
From their climax.

Hectic virgin fury rinsed with dew;
Red nerves; white lust!—If you
Could only keep in jewel-case
The word, the face.

To see you pull upon each other's flesh,
And how you strain the mesh,
I fear eventual narrow bed
In which you'll wed.

46

You group your bodies like old potter's ware,
Moulded that people stare,
And placed on chimney-piece apart
To please their heart.

I hope you'll not be thwarted in your lust
Now while you so trust.
You are too like that vernal green,
Once only seen.

Here is an orchard. While the fruit be sweet
Pluck all you can, and eat.
So many lovers mix like you,
But which are true?

A WORD

HAVE you ever loved a word
Better than the man who spoke it?
So the moment that you heard
Its delightful syllables
Fall upon the air
You went wandering idly home
Dreaming of the way it cooled
That uncomfortable room?
Trying to repeat it slowly
Standing back from it and watching
Like a lover
To discover
What it meant and why you loved it.

Mostly words like hailstones tumble
On the thin air and disperse
In indiscriminating jumble
Incoherent or perverse.

Why did you speak this evening
Suddenly like that
Just as I was going?

THE QUIET MIND

IN my small room
I wonder, oh, how much I wonder how
I, born, can think, and see and feel, and hear
Till my quiet mind does whisper to my ear
I'm yours; you're mine. Be sure you're true to me.
I'm joy, I'm life, friend and Eternity.

CROSSING A BRIDGE

THAT bridge has never yet been measured;
It is more long than any bridge before.
Daylong, nightlong, yearlong, nightmare-long
There is a crossing of it, and a roar
Of oily-livered engines which to feed
Ten million tanks drip their explosive fumes
Threading a vibrant romp of speed.
Crossing a bridge; crossing a bridge: that's all.

They are not sure of what they have to do
Except they know that they must stamp their way
Through time, leave time behind them, beat the day,
Leave it behind, leave everything; go, go
Forward, away, grind, screw, drive, thrash, compel,
Cleave, grapple, shoot toward the other end.
There rings; there rings an everlasting bell:

A summons; an alarm; a drive; a call,
A cry beyond an iron unopened door;
Or knuckles flapping on a hollow wall;
Or in a cage, a roar;
Or in a desert no escape to hills;
Or in a valley, longing for the sea:
A strangled rush of overmastered wills
Imagining a chance of being free.

A DREAM

THE first time I rang,
Oh, loud you cried.
The second time, they answered:
"She has died."

"Died!" I cried: "Died? Died? Died?"
The telephone emptily, emptily sighed.
"Death, will you answer, please?"
—"Yes, she has died."

DISILLUSIONMENT

WHEN all our words have gone too far
  And cannot well retract;
While all the deeds we swore we'd do
  Are flowing into act.
Then we will pick our bodies up
  Deliberately try
But on the point of trying best
  We bend ourselves and die.

So when you ramble making all
  The promises you must,
Remember that your pledge is but
  From dust and unto dust,
And every brave delightful oath
  You make for being true
Is mortgaged and disqualified
  By coming out of you.

You speak because a little thought
  Is rambling through your brain,
And, on the verge of death, you fear
  You may not talk again.
Oh, large delightful power of speech
  I'm tired because of you:
Oh, wild ideal of swearing well
  What you can never do.

I'll go away this very night
  And leave my comrades here
And never talk to them again
  Who trust me and are dear.

We who have passed the ancient state
  Of speculating brain
We'll drink a glass and part and pass
  And never hope again.

TO THE LADIES OF THE CONVENT

THEY do exist; for I have seen their House.
An ugly structure, gothic-windowed, hard,
Pale, gaunt and plain, brick-built, with slated roof,
Surrounded by thin brick-builded wall,
Enclosed discreetly by a lean old hedge of
Rustling yews that meditate on dust.

Who are they, who, within, not ever seen,
Commune upon the silence of their God?
He will not speak; nor ever spoke to-day.
Their floating Prayer has become a kind
Of vague enticement to an absent love.

But as I pass this Convent I can't help
Dreaming about their virgin thought of Him.
If they should come outside into the world,
Maybe he would be wandering down the Strand,
Or strolling into Piccadilly Circus.

O, chimèd, secret, formal discipline!
Forgive me that I pause and gently laugh.
Great oceans of the breaking buttercup
Yellow, incestuous, without any care
Are foaming over pasture to your wall.

You can't defeat this imminent attack,
Summer is raging through the frantic country;
Thorn, may, and elder breed gigantic hedgerows
Sprouting across indefinite wild limits,
Spreading themselves like fools and never asking:
Lilac; laburnum: with their sudden ending,
Great, large and terrible, like something doomed.

I know the cold delight you have upon you.
You give so little, but receive for ever.
Conscience is like a policeman in your cells.

It would be strange if you could lie among them,
Press your chilled temples closely to their bodies.
Be like an everlasting understanding,
Be like the God you have so blindly worshipped,
Be like a buttercup, a mustard seed,
Or field of pasture: How the silk would rustle.
Black-robes, give up your bodies for a moment.

But the tall bricks that wall you are too safe.
The yews, the cypresses, the crucifix.
You will remain upon your virgin beds
Dreaming of sweet Communion holy bright,
Harmless, and comfortably always right.
Sure there is harm in night, which you are: Night.

SAFE PASSAGE

THE stream of traffic flowed along the street.
We waited at the corner—whom to meet?

In this gigantic town, plain life should be
Simpler than most remote simplicity—
But in the turmoil of this unreal town
With parched hard tongue and face turned dustward down
One lies and tries to hold one's gulp of breath
Fighting so feebly against calm death.

I would so like Life to die, if only
One did not think too much of being lonely,
And of the large and angry forms that rise
All night·in dreams and fill their hopeless skies.

GOD OF DOGS

CLEARLY the news has reached us from the skies
Man has no faithful Master always wise,
But dogs are different—Not a dog but can
Believe in one dear God and Master-Man,
Dog has a leash and automatic food
And clear decision for eventual good.
He prays and he is answered. When his creed
Fails him he makes another to his need.
A fortunate reserve of heavenly power
Provides him with a use for every hour.
O, happy dog he cares not to foresee
Eventualities of eternity.
His movements dream through plain existent Now;
No speculations crease his hairy brow,
In his great white religion he can hide
His soul, in its perfectitude abide.

Kick is so swiftly followed by caress,
Sorrow so soon forgotten in blessedness.
He is not tempted ever that he swerve
From the first purpose patiently to serve.
Ask!—He can love. Look!—but he cannot kneel.
Wonder at him!—Oh, what can Dog not feel!
Think if your confident mind of deity can
Of what he must have left, to come to Man

The swift desirousness of chase by scent
The early ways his natural instinct went—
Watch him discovered in his ancient mood
Brought back to kennel from some park or wood.
See the wild glint in his repentant eyes,
His yap which broke across the grass in cries
Is turned now almost to uncanny tears.
And yet he loves far better than he fears.
His wide eyes change their colour. All his nerves
Move to your hand. His sense not ever swerves
Out of belief. He, patient, loving, true,
Whatever God may purpose or may do,
Follows and will obey. . . .
                                    O, happy beast
Try not to become too wise,
Restrain yourself from mysteries;
Revere your God, respect his laws,
You must not hope to know their cause.
Dog, be a dog contentedly!
Dog, always be my dog to me.
I want no human friend but do
Not ever make me forfeit you.

PLACARDS

THEY shriek or like huddled birds
They sing
Reminding us all how we must be
Remembering.

Stiff or swinging with hard square corners
They jerk a tremendous word
Into our eyes. It rings like a bell.—
Enough! We have heard!

But they urge unsparingly. Every space
Is filled. Through the whole wide town
The crouching springing newsboys race,
And chase the public down.

Three dozen times as I cross the road
I have seen the same and the same
Till the news has crawled on my back like a load
Or become like the burden of my own name.

Let it be finished! They shout and glare
Like fallen sky-signs, they flicker and flare,
They float like flags in Trafalgar Square,

They are carried like trays and brought to my feet;
Everywhere is a newsboy's beat—
The main street. The side street.

In red, in blue, in black, in green;
Is there no space to pass between?

Which of us has asked to know
The news in every path he go?

Let us be pilgrims. We will go
To a distant land where news is slow.

Let us be hermits. We will wait
Carefully the call of Fate.

FRAGMENT

WHO talked of God? Who talked of peace?
  Or the great next Great War to come?
Who talked of times when war shall cease,
  And men walk slowly home?

I heard a jabbering mass of tongues
  Expending words on brilliant air;
Through flashing lips I heard great lungs
  Proclaiming courage mighty fair.

Gigantic vanities low sprang
  And captured by the flimsy hair
That innocence whose quick cries rang
  To nowhere through enormous air.

The Vast Directors growled and spumed,
  The sirens from the Factories shrieked,
And all the Earth was vaguely fumed
  Drenched with calm smoke, and coned, and streaked.

I held my hands back to my heart
  And watched like someone at a show
Who waits dispassionately apart
  For what the unknown dice may throw.

Then suddenly from out my dreams
  A great God furiously appeared.
"The World is not," he said, "what seems;
  "This World is not what you have feared."

Then cosily I settled down,
  Thinking: An idle dream I've had,
Yet all my body waxed in frown;
  Are dreams so mad? Are dreams so mad?

        .   .   .   .   .

I spring to life from out the dark.
  Is new illumination sent?
Some God is—if all men could hark—
  Through private vision vaguely blent.

He will not visit me to-night,
  To-morrow, or another day;
But He, thank Him, will re-appear
  In all I do, or think, or say.

I'm stupid, yet I'm better far
  Than He, and He will never know
This all consuming avatar
  In which I am, and live, and grow.

        .   .   .   .   .

I'm worried, God, by your pale voice.
  You are unlike us. We to-day
In our own anxious flesh rejoice,
  Deaf to whatever you can say.

57

Ring your old thunder: we won't hear.
  String lightning: we have got that down.
It is no good if you draw near.
  We're settled in our final town.

No wireless you can now contrive,
  Old Patriarch, will make us seem
More than we are, that is, alive,
  Dependent on an anxious dream.

PRAYER TO MEMORY

WHY have you veiled your eyes?
Why are you dumbed by the power of
  your own thought?

You know all, know all.
Yet a man may toil through his life
Unavailingly, unfruitfully trying
To gather one hint from your lips.

O, give me a token!
I do not believe in the braggart
Who boasts of vague beauty remembered,
But never has looked upon You.

When a man has abandoned thought
And returned to his daily labour,
Then you uncover your eyes,
And your thrilling voice
Will ring through the meadows of time.

"Memory spoke to me, spoke to me,"
A man will cry as from sleep;
But, before he can capture their sound,
Your words will have drifted away, away.
He may know indeed the ring of your voice,
But no clue will remain in his mind.

.   .   .   .   .

Memory, mother of thought,
Help me!
I am a child of the past;
Heir to the future: you hold
Both of these in your brain.

You can look forward and backward:
You can combine
Future and past into one,
So that you govern the world.

I implore:
May your words
Ring more clearly, more clearly,
Ring through my heart and my brain,
That I rejoice in the Earth.

THE SILENT POOL

I

I HAVE discovered finally to-day
This house that I have called my own
Is built of straw and clay,
Not, as I thought, of stone.

I wonder who the architect could be,
What builder made it of that stuff;
When it was left to me
The house seemed good enough.

Yet, slowly, as its roof began to sink,
And as its walls began to split,
And I began to think,
Then I suspected it;

But did not clearly know until to-day
That it was only built of straw and clay.

II

Now I will go about on my affairs
As though I had no cares,
Nor ever think at all
How one day soon that house is bound to fall,
So when I'm told the wind has blown it down
I may have something else to call my own.

I have enquired who was the architect,
What builder did erect.
I'm told they did design
Million and million others all like mine,
And argument with all men ends the same:—
It is impossible to fix the blame.

I am so glad that underneath our talk
Our minds together walk.
We argue all the while,
But down below our argument we smile.
We have our houses, but we understand
That our real property is common land.

At night we often go
With happy comrades to that real estate,
Where dreams in beauty grow,
And every man enjoys a common fate.

At night in sleep one flows
Below the surface of all argument;
The brain, with all it knows,
Is covered by the waters of content.

But when the dawn appears
Brain rises to the surface with a start,
And, waking, quickly sneers
At the old natural brightness of the heart.

Oh, that a man might choose
To live unconsciously like beast or bird,
And our clear thought not loose
Its beauty when we turn it into word.

IV

Those quarrellings between my brain and heart
(In which I'd take no part)
Pursue their violent course
Corrupting my most vital force
So that my natural property is spent
In fees to keep alive their argument.

V

Look downward in the silent pool:
The weeds cling to the ground they love;

They live so quietly, are so cool;
They do not need to think, or move.

Look down in the unconscious mind:
There everything is quiet too
And deep and cool, and you will find
Calm growth and nothing hard to do,
And nothing that need trouble you.

ONE MOMENT ONLY

WHAT river do we walk beside,
So red and strong and throbbing like a heart?—
O Brain, now you and I
Are dreaming of the river of all Blood.

Dive from this bank, and I will follow;
And we will swim against the current up.
Plunge! Ah, do not awaken:
Loud the blood flows. Strike upward to the source.

Hold me!—You must not tire;
For you and I will talk of this, years after;
We shall remember it for ever.
I am so happy now.

.   .   .   .   .

You're failing, failing. We shall drown.
Where are you? I have lost you in the dark.
Oh, the thick blood is roaring through my body.
Into what world have I awakened now?
Brain, could you not have dreamed a little longer?

EARTHLINESS

How can I tell,
I who now live,
What I have been in the past before I was born?

Memory cries,
Heart can repeat
Echo of echo from cave after cave of my life.

I can imagine,
Stretching my thought
Backward and backward, my fathers, their fathers, and theirs,

And the one long
Faithful desire
Driving through ages to me who am breathing and here.

But as I burrow
Deep into Mind,
Only the dark passage widens: I can't feel the walls.

Oh, there must be,
Somewhere beyond,
Through all that darkness, a light, for there's often a sound,

That roars in my ears
Like waves on the rocks
Of an ocean I've known, and when I remember that life

Then in my body,
Or in my heart,
Or in my brain, some quarrel, or hunger or love,

Cruel, too great
To be hidden, too eager,
Too wild for the tame life we live, will arise and cry;

Suddenly shriek,
As one who has been
Buried alive, awak'ning, might shriek in the earth:

Calling and calling,
Shaking my body,
Till I unbury the dead and discover the past.

.   .   .   .   .

Soul, oh my soul,
Here is your master,
God and begetter, yes hundred-fold father. He lives

Deep in your flesh,
Soul of my body, O Soul:
You must be faithful to him. He is God unto you.

If he is wild
Is he not you?
If he is wanton, not you? If rebellious, not you?

In the young world,
Out of the sea,
Slowly he crept with you, feeling his way to the sun;

And in the light,
High on the beach,
Laid down your body, and moulded the shape of you,
      Soul:

All that long time,
Low in your ear,
Whispered the spells of the earth, which you heard not at first.

Slowly, the slow,
Slowly and slowly, the sound,
Sound of his whispering moulded your ear to his voice.

     .   .   .   .   .

Lift up your head
Over the hills:
The distance is filled with the image and shadow of him;

Of him, and of him,
Like a forest, an ocean,
A mountain, a world.
             But who is it speaks in me now?

Who is it speaks?
Is it my brain?
Who was it talking within me and to me at once?

Silence replies,
And no one can tell
The voice from the silence, or knows when the Voice shall
    begin.

UNDERWORLD

THE vaults down in the underworld are not so dumb as
    they would seem
To us who walk above them with our feet upon their roofs.

For the shapeless is for ever groping back to form: the dead
    make sounds
Like pebbles falling in a pool, or roots that hope to reach the
    water,
Stretching out, and writhing out, and moaning out.

There is no end among the corridors below: they wind about
    the world;
And shadows flow along them and are whispering through-
    out them.
Or slowly from the far-away a rumour will come floating
(Through cavern after cavern) of a dark tumultuous struggle:
Spirits forming from the shapeless, called by Time and
    taking journey.
Eyes are sealed, and voices wordless: they have just begun to
    wonder
What Body means, where Light can be: their nerves are
    feeling forward.
They are groping at their roof:
How they strive to force their hands up,
Crawling over mounds of skulls
To the tender thrilling surface.
There are shadows there of shadows. There are images and
    spectres
That make shadows on the high earth: ghosts invisible to eyes
Too accustomed to the daylight. But by looking inward,
    backward
In the pool of mind, and leaning
To that place of inward shadows,
Where the world is like a spectre,
You can feel among the turnings and the spaces of the
    underworld,
And help the groping spirits in to thought. Now they will
    wonder:—

"What was that? What are those feet I hear?
Who moves above my head? Why is that distant earth so
    white and clear,
And filled with strong vibration? I will learn to make a body,
And to move myself about."
You can lead their ghostly movings.
They will waken into form. They will make a world about
    them.
They will walk if you desire them.

FATE

I

I HAVE so often
Examined all this well-known room
That I inhabit.

There is the open window;
There the locked door, the door I cannot open,
The only doorway.

When at the keyhole often, often
I bend and listen, I can always hear
A muffled conversation.

An argument:
An angry endless argument of people
Who live behind;

Some loudly talking,
Some dimly into separate conflict moving,
Behind the door.

There they seem prisoned,
As I, in this lone room that I inhabit:
My life; my body.

You, of the previous Being,
You who once made me, and who now discuss me,
Tell me your edict.

You, long ago,
With doubting hands and eager trembling fingers,
Prepared my room.

Before I came,
Each gave a token for remembrance, left it,
And then retired behind the bolted door.

There is the pot of honey
One brought, and there the jar of vinegar
On the same table.

Who poured that water
Shining beside the flask of yellow wine?
Who sighed so softly?

Who brought that living flower to the room?
Who groaned—and I can ever hear the echo?
—You do not answer.

Meanwhile from out the distance
Sounds reach me as of building other houses:
Men building houses.

And if they ever
Should open up a doorway in the wall,
And I pass onward,

What should I take them
Beyond those doorways, in the other rooms?
What shall I bring them,
That they may love me?

Fatal question!
For all the jangling voices rise together:
"What should he take them?"

"What shall he take them?"
Through that locked door there is no final answer.
They are debating, endlessly debating. . . .

II

O Fate! Have you no other gift
Than voices in a muffled room?
Why do you live behind a door,
And hide yourself in gloom?

And why, again, should you not have
One purpose only, one sole word,
Ringing for ever round my heart:
Plainly delivered, plainly heard?

Your conversation fills my brain
And tortures all my life, and yet
Gives nothing, and I often think
You've grown so old, that you forget;

And having learnt man's fatal trick
Of talking, talking, talking still,
You're tired of definite design,
And laugh at having lost your Will.

GRAVITY

I

F IT for perpetual worship is the power
That holds our bodies safely to the earth.

When people talk of their domestic gods,
Then privately I think of You.

We ride through space upon your shoulders
Conveniently and lightly set,
And, so accustomed, we relax our hold,
Forget the gentle motion of your body—
But You do not forget.

Sometimes you breathe a little faster,
Or move a muscle:
Then we remember you, O Master.

II

While people meet in reverent groups
And sing to their domestic God,
You, all that time, dear tyrant (How I laugh!)
Could, without effort, place your hand among them,
And sprinkle them.

But all your ways are carefully ordered,
For you have never questioned duty.
We watch your everlasting combinations;
We call them fate; we turn them to our pleasure,
And when they most delight us, call them beauty.

I rest my body on your grass,
And let my brain repose in you:
I feel these living moments pass,
And, from within myself to those far places
To be imagined in your time and spaces,
Deliberate the various acts you do :—

Sorting and re-arranging worlds of Matter
Keenly and wisely. Thus you brought our earth
Through stages, and from purpose back to purpose;
From fire to fog, to dust, to birth
Through beast to man, who led himself to brain—
(And you will draw him back to dust again.)

By leave of you he places stone on stone;
He scatters seed: you are at once the prop
Among the long roots of his fragile crop.
You manufacture for him, and insure
House, harvest, implement and furniture,
And hold them all secure.

IV

The hill. . . . The trees. . . . From underneath
I feel You pull me with your hand:
Through my firm feet up to my heart
You hold me,—You are in the land,
Reposing underneath the hill.

You keep my balance and my growth.
I lift a foot, but where I go
You follow: you, the ever-strong,
Control the smallest thing I do.

If by some little human power
I turn your purpose to my end,
For that I thank you every hour.
I stand at worship, while you send
Thrills up my body to my heart,
And I am all in love to know
How by your strength you keep me part
Of earth, which cannot let me go;
How everything I see around,
Whether it can or cannot move,
Is granted liberty of ground,
And freedom to enjoy your love;

Though you are silent always, and, alone
To You yourself, your power remains unknown.

THE GARDEN

HE told me he had seen a ruined garden
Outside the town.
"Where? Where?"
I asked him quickly.
He said it lay toward the southern country;
He knew the road well: he would take me there.

Then he sat down and talked
About that garden.
He was so grandly proud and sure of it,
I listened all the evening to his talk.

And our glasses were emptied,
Talking of it.

We filled them and filled them again,
Talking of it.

He said that no one knew
The garden but himself;
Though hundreds passed it day by day,
Yet no one knew it but himself.

I

The garden, it was long and wide
And filled with great unconscious peace;
All the old trees were tall and large,
And all the birds—

The birds, he said, were like a choir
Of lively boys,
Who never went to school,
But sang instead.

He told me of the trailing flowers
Hung on the ruined walls;
The rivers and their waterfalls;
The hidden woods; the lawns; the bowers.

Small cool plantations; palm and vine,
With fig-tree growing by their side,
And violet and maidenhair
And

II

we were late in conversation
Talking of that most wonderful garden,
And filled our glasses again and again
Talking about that beautiful garden,

Until he vowed in the middle of drink
To lead me to-morrow to see it myself.
We closed our hands on the pact.
He vanished away through the dark.

III

To-morrow, to-morrow, we start our walk.
To-morrow is here and he meets me surely.
Out from the city we go and pursue
Mile after mile of the open road;

Come to a place of sudden trees,
Pass it across the fields, then on
By farmyards, through villages, over the downs:

Mile after mile we walk. He is pleased.
Our feet become heavy with dust, and we laugh,
And we talk all the while of our future delight.

IV

He came upon the garden in the dusk;
He leaned against the wall:
He pointed out its beauties in the gloom.
We lay down weary in the shadow of elms,
And stared between their branches at the moon,
And talked about to-morrow and the garden.
I knew that everything he said was true,
For we were resting up against the wall.

V

Oh hard awakening from a dream:
I thought I was in paradise.

He cooked the coffee we had brought,
Then looked about him.

We had not reached the wall, he found.
It was a little farther on.
We walked another mile or two,
And stood before the ruined gate.

He was not satisfied at all.
He said the entrance was not here.
I hardly understood his talk,
And so I watched him move about.
Indeed, it was the garden he had meant;
But not the one he had described.

VI

Then suddenly from out his conversation
I saw it in the light of his own thought:
A phantom Eden shining
Placid among his dreams.

And he, with large eyes and with hands uplifted,
Cried: "Look, O look!" Indeed I saw the garden;
The ghostly palm and violet,
Fig, maidenhair, and fountain;

The rivers and their flowered lawns; the gleaming
Birds; and their song—I heard that clear I know.
And silent, in amazement,
We stared

Then both sat down beneath the wall and rested,
And in our conversation
Lived in the garden.

VII

"We'll come again next week," he said at last.
"We have no leisure to explore it now;
Besides we cannot climb this crumbling wall:
Our gate is on the farther side, I know.
We'd have to go right round, and even then
I am not sure it's open till the spring.
I have affairs in town. If you don't mind,
We will go back directly. After all,
The garden cannot run away, or change.
Next week I'll have more time, and, once inside,
Who knows . . . who knows? How very curious too,
Hundreds of people pass it day by day
Along that high road over there; the cars—
Look at them! And the railway too! Well. Well,
I'm glad that no one cares for Eden now.
It would be spoilt so quickly. We'll go back
By train, if you don't mind. I've walked enough.
Look, there's the station.   Eh?"

VIII

I did not see that man again
Until a year had gone or more.
I had not found him anywhere,
And many times had gone to seek
The garden, but it was not there.

One day along the country road
There was he coming all alone.
He would have passed me with a stare.
I held his arm, but he was cold,

And rudely asked me my affair.
I said, there was a garden, I'd been told . . .

IX

Then suddenly came that rapture upon us;
We saw the garden again in our mutual thought:
Blue and yellow and green,
Shining by day or by night.

"Those are the trees," he said, "and there is the gateway.
To-day, I think, it is open. And shall we not go there?"
Quickly we ran in our joy;
Quickly—then stopped, and stared.

X

An angel with a flaming sword
Stood large, and beautiful, and clear:
He covered up his golden eyes,
And would not look as we came near.

Birds wheeled about the flowery gate,
But we could never see inside,
Although (I often think) it stood
Slack on its hinges open wide.

The angel dropped his hopeless sword,
And stood with his great pinions furled,
And wept into his hands: but we
Feared, and turned back to our own world.

77

SPRING

I

A SHADOW by the cottage door.
Not you to-day. You have taken wings:—
Out of the burning bush a bird
Has found you: to his mate he sings.
The battlements of paradise
Are taken at a single note.
Two pirouetting butterflies
Fall from the sky:
You change; you float,
In their love-chase, a butterfly.
Where they have circled, quivering wheels
Of yellow, for a moment, light
The track of your impetuous flight. . . .
O now what tenement will suit
Your choice?
Will you be thistledown,
And, in the currents of the wind,
Swim all about the air,
Then dive and find
A chink in earth and warmly nestle there?
Or will you lower
Your voice,
And join the honey-laden undertone,
Murmuring a moment in a flower,
Then zumming to another and another?
Or cast all wings
And burrow in the ground
Where blind and glossy creeping coiling things
Love without sound
Among the roots? . . .

I wait. The undulating trill
Breaks in a tournament of song.
The rut, in every changing thrill,
Grips and becomes more strong,
As, with a breath, or by a kiss,
It makes the microcosm stir,
Warm under shell or chrysalis,
Dissolves the bud, designs the wing,
Adorns the body in its fur,
And passes into everything
From underground, and up the trees,
And over them and far away,
Through clouds among the flying storms
That gather in their separate forms,
Bend down upon their shining knees,
Festoon their rainbows on the brow
Of Earth, and garland it in spray.
I follow. You have vanished now
Down slimy rocks among the seas.

The darting fish remembers too,
And pranks a gaudy fin to please;
Flashes him forth to fight a place
Among the ancients of the race.

You know the sound of clanking scales.
Your memory begins to creep
Through the cold blood of dreamy-eyed
Old monsters, rising from their sleep.
It is your pilgrimage to fill
The world in all its tracks and trails.

I follow you along the river-side,
Out to the meadowland and up the hill,
Among your flowers, back into your wood,
Where first we stood . . .
What can you show me more?
Under your wings I stare. . . . And is there still
A shadow by the cottage door?

III

Where you have built your wandering paradise
We always follow you.
That single moment that you give
Blossoms in endless tracks on sea and shore,
The current of desire to live,
The lust to grip a single moment more.
We can but follow you,
And when you bargain we must pay the price.

Then, homely, at the last you lead us round
Into the place where we have been before,
By different ways along familiar ground,
Into the shadow of a cottage door.

INTROSPECTION

THAT house across the road is full of ghosts;
The windows, all inquisitive, look inward:
All are shut.
I've never seen a body in the house;

Have you? Have you?
Yet feet go sounding in the corridors,
And up and down, and up and down the stairs,
All day, all night, all day.

When will the show begin?
When will the host be in?
What is the preparation for?
When will he open the bolted door?
When will the minutes move smoothly along in their hours?
Time, answer!

The air must be hot: how hot inside.
If only somebody could go
And snap the windows open wide,
And keep them so!

All the back rooms are very large, and there
(So it is said)
They sit before their open books and stare;
Or one will rise and sadly shake his head;
Another will but comb and comb her hair,
While some will move untiringly about
Through all the rooms, for ever in and out,
Or up and down the stair;

Or gaze into the small back-garden
And talk about the rain,
Then drift back from the window to the table,
Folding long hands, to sit and think again.

They do never meet like homely people
Round a fireside
After daily work . . .

Always busy with procrastination,
Backward and forward they move in the house,
Full of their questions
No one can answer.
Nothing will happen.... Nothing will happen....

REAL PROPERTY

TELL *me about that harvest field.*
Oh! Fifty acres of living bread.
The colour has painted itself in my heart.
The form is patterned in my head.

So now I take it everywhere;
See it whenever I look round;
Hear it growing through every sound,
Know exactly the sound it makes—
Remembering, as one must all day,
Under the pavement the live earth aches.

Trees are at the farther end,
Limes all full of the mumbling bee:
So there must be a harvest field
Whenever one thinks of a linden tree.

A hedge is about it, very tall,
Hazy and cool, and breathing sweet.
Round paradise is such a wall
And all the day, in such a way,
In paradise the wild birds call.

You only need to close your eyes
And go within your secret mind,
And you'll be into paradise:
I've learnt quite easily to find
Some linden trees and drowsy bees,
A tall sweet hedge with the corn behind.

I will not have that harvest mown:
I'll keep the corn and leave the bread.
I've bought that field; it's now my own:
I've fifty acres in my head.
I take it as a dream to bed.
I carry it about all day. . . .

Sometimes when I have found a friend
I give a blade of corn away.

OUTSIDE EDEN

Adam

HOW glad I am to think that our idle life is finished for
    ever.
 I forbid you to loiter round the Gate. There is work for you,
    my woman.
I always wanted to be an honest respectable man.
And I hated dawdling about under the trees all day
Nibbling bananas and sucking grapes. Look at that cave in
    the hill.
That is our future home, and you must learn to cook.
The world is a different place. The sooner you know it the
    better.

83

Eve

Eden! Eden! How the sun
Is glittering on the garden still.
Adam! Adam! You are changed.
Oh the black cave, the sullen hill.

Adam

The cave is for you, for me the hill. Be sure you remember
    that.
Here in the World the beasts of the World devour and are
    devoured.
Here you will have no more silky lions, tame leopards and
    hornless bulls.
This is my club, this tree; and you must hide in that cave.
I shall go hunt for your meat: you will find it much wiser
    food
Than apples.

Eve

O my lord, you're changed.
I wish I had not learnt to sin.
Morning and night I'll pray and pray:
Perhaps at last He'll let us in.

Adam

Shame! Shame! You are thinking once more of your
    peacocks and swans and goldfish.
You're only an idle woman; no wife for an honest man.
If ever you try to return I'll pray to God that He kill you.

Is not our cave a good enough home? I have longed for it all
    my life.
Here we can plan the world: a useful world for our sons.

Eve

And was not Eden useful too?
Did God not plan it for his men?
How short our time was in that land.
We are not happy now as then.

Adam

Well. Well. Just settle down. I'll be as kind as I can.
You're only a woman after all. You need my protection.
    Don't cry.
Everyone sooner or later must learn to know the World.
Eden was only a holiday. Now there is life, great Life.
You try to kindle a fire, while I must go down to the river.
Work is the future law; Work to keep one alive;
Work to forget one's life with. . . .

Eve

Work is the only law!
Dreadful law and sad.
To work, to work will be good:
To idle will be bad.

So our children will learn
The ways of evil and good.
The Evil shall have no meat:
The Righteous shall have their
    food.

85

I

IN lonely silence
Of windless country
I think of those
In far London
Who move in lamplight.

Hark!—the shuffle
Of groping feet.
No—the branches
Keen at the window.

II

I heard the latch:
You have gone perhaps
To buy food in the town.

It must have been that,
By the way the old house
Becomes suddenly quiet
Like a dog awaiting
Its absent master.

III

Look! Look!
Those are the fields
Of Paradise. . . .

—What can you mean?
That is the pasture,
The pond, the cattle,
(Grazing by moonlight),
Of my old tenant,
Mister Brown.

IV

The moonlight, it was blowing in waves
To-night when I crossed the fields:
I waited below by the hedge.

My breath was caught up by the wind ;
I stood and expected to drown.

Curling across the green,
It folded me up:
I swam to the land,
Came back to the house,
In the shelter of trees,
To the safety of you.

DOG

O LITTLE friend, your nose is ready; you sniff,
Asking for that expected walk,
(Your nostrils full of the happy rabbit-whiff)
And almost talk.

And so the moment becomes a moving force;
Coats glide down from their pegs in the humble dark;

You scamper the stairs,
Your body informed with the scent and the track and the
    mark
Of stoats and weasels, moles and badgers and hares.

We are going *Out*. You know the pitch of the word,
Probing the tone of thought as it comes through fog
And reaches by devious means (half-smelt, half-heard)
The four-legged brain of a walk-ecstatic dog.

Out through the garden your head is already low.
You are going your walk, you know,
And your limbs will draw
Joy from the earth through the touch of your padded
    paw.

Now, sending a little look to us behind,
Who follow slowly the track of your lovely play,
You fetch our bodies forward away from mind
Into the light and fun of your useless day.

.   .   .   .   .

Thus, for your walk, we took ourselves, and went
Out by the hedge, and tree, to the open ground.
You ran, in delightful strata of wafted scent,
Over the hill without seeing the view;
Beauty is hinted through primitive smells to you:
And that ultimate Beauty you track is but rarely found.

.   .   .   .   .

Home . . . and further joy will be waiting there:
Supper full of the lovely taste of bone.
You lift up your nose again, and sniff, and stare
For the rapture known

Of the quick wild gorge of food, then the still lie-down;
While your people will talk above you in the light
Of candles, and your dreams will merge and drown
Into the bed-delicious hours of night.

GOLDFISH

THEY are the angels of that watery world.
All innocent, they no more than aspire
To move themselves about on golden fins.
Or they can fill their paradise with fire
By darting suddenly from end to end.

Their eyes stare out from far away behind,
And cannot pierce the barrier of Mind.
In the same house are they and we;
Yet well might be
Divided by a whole Eternity.

When twilight flows across the evening room
And air becomes like water, you can feel
Their movements growing larger in the gloom,
And merging with the room, and you are brought
Back where they live, the other side of thought.

Then in the morning, when the seven rays
Of London sunlight one by one incline,
They glide to meet them, and their gulping lips
Suck the light in, so they are caught and played
Like salmon on a heavenly fishing line.

89

THISTLEDOWN

THIS might have been a place for sleep
But, as from that small hollow there
Hosts of bright thistledown begin
Their dazzling journey through the air,
An idle man can only stare.

They grip their withered edge of stalk
In brief excitement for the wind;
They hold a breathless final talk,
And when their filmy cables part
One almost hears a little cry.

Some cling together while they wait
And droop and gaze and hesitate,
But others leap along the sky,
Or circle round and calmly choose
The gust they know they ought to use.

While some in loving pairs will glide,
Or watch the others as they pass,
Or rest on flowers in the grass,
Or circle through the shining day
Like silvery butterflies at play.

Some catch themselves to every mound,
Then lingeringly and slowly move
As if they knew the precious ground
Were opening for their fertile love:
They almost try to dig, they need
So much to plant their thistle-seed.

THE NIGHTINGALE NEAR THE HOUSE

HERE is the soundless cypress on the lawn:
It listens, listens. Taller trees beyond
Listen. The moon at the unruffled pond
    Stares. And you sing, you sing.

That star-enchanted song falls through the air
From lawn to lawn down terraces of sound,
Darts in white arrows on the shadowed ground;
    While all the night you sing.

My dreams are flowers to which you are a bee,
As all night long I listen, and my brain
Receives your song, then loses it again
    In moonlight on the lawn.

Now is your voice a marble high and white,
Then like a mist on fields of paradise;
Now is a raging fire, then is like ice,
    Then breaks, and it is dawn.

CITY-STORM

THE heavy sounds are over-sweet
That droop above the hooded street,
At any moment ripe to fall and lie,
And when that Wind will swagger up the town
They'll bend a moment, then will fly
All clattering down.

Troupes come and go of urchin breeze;
They flick your face or smack the trees,
Then round the corner spin and leap
With whistling cries,
Rake their rubbish in a heap
And throw it in your eyes.

(Much preparation of the earth and air
Is needed everywhere
Before that first large drop of rain can fall.)

Smells of the Sea, or inland Grass,
Come staring through the town and pass.
Brilliant old Memories drive in state
Along the way, but cannot wait;
And many a large unusual bird
Hovers across the sky half-heard.
But listen. It is He;
At last he comes:
Gigantic tyrant panting through the street,
Slamming the windows of our little homes,
Banging the doors, knocking the chimneys down.
Oh, his loud tramp: how scornfully he can meet
Great citizens, and lash them with his sleet!
Everything will be altered in our town.

He'll wipe the film of habit clean away.
While he remains,
His cloak is over everything we do,
And the whole town complains:—

A sombre scroll;
An inner room.
A crystal bowl:
Waters of gloom.

Oh, the darkened house—
Into silence creep!
The world is cold.
All people weep.

UNKNOWN COUNTRY

HERE, in this other world, they come and go
With easy dream-like movements to and fro.
They stare through lovely eyes, yet do not seek
An answering gaze, or that a man should speak.
Had I a load of gold, and should I come
Bribing their friendship, and to buy a home,
They would stare harder and would slightly frown:
I am a stranger from the distant town.

Oh, with what patience I have tried to win
The favour of the hostess of the Inn!
Have I not offered toast on frothing toast
Looking toward the melancholy host;
Praised the old wall-eyed mare to please the groom;
Laughed to the laughing maid and fetched her broom;
Stood in the background not to interfere
When the cool ancients frolicked at their beer;
Talked only in my turn, and made no claim
For recognition or by voice or name,
Content to listen, and to watch the blue
Or grey of eyes, or what good hands can do?

Sun-freckled lads, who at the dusk of day
Stroll through the village with a scent of hay
Clinging about you from the windy hill,

Why do you keep your secret from me still?
You loiter at the corner of the street:
I in the distance silently entreat.
I know too well I'm city-soiled, but then
So are to-day ten million other men.
My heart is true: I've neither will nor charms
To lure away your maidens from your arms.
Trust me a little. Must I always stand
Lonely, a stranger from an unknown land?

There is a riddle here. Though I'm more wise
Than you, I cannot read your simple eyes.
I find the meaning of their gentle look
More difficult than any learned book.
I pass: perhaps a moment you may chaff
My walk, and so dismiss me with a laugh.
I come: you all, most grave and most polite,
Stand silent first, then wish me calm Good-Night.
When I go back to town some one will say:
"I think that stranger must have gone away."
And "Surely!" some one else will then reply.
Meanwhile, within the dark of London, I
Shall, with my forehead resting on my hand,
Not cease remembering your distant land;
Endeavouring to reconstruct aright
How some treed hill has looked in evening light;
Or be imagining the blue of skies
Now as in heaven, now as in your eyes;
Or in my mind confusing looks or words
Of yours with dawnlight, or the song of birds:
Not able to resist, not even keep
Myself from hovering near you in my sleep:
You still as callous to my thought and me
As flowers to the purpose of bee.

94

WHILE WE SLEEP

THE earth takes up our bodies, every one,
And brings them slowly backward to the dark;
Then on her shadowed side we droop and slumber,
Turned from the sun.

(Meanwhile He covers continents in light
One after other, so they stretch and wake,
Live their day through and droop again to slumber:
Day, night: day, night.)

The stars shine forth and disappear again,
Roaring about in space above our heads,
While we are folded to the earth in slumber
With dreaming brain.

We travel through the darkness: we are spun
Upward through rays of light into the morning;
We waken with the earth: we glide from slumber
Toward the sun.

MAN CARRYING BALE

THE tough hand closes gently on the load;
    Out of the mind, a voice
Calls "Lift!" and the arms, remembering well their work,
    Lengthen and pause for help.

Then a slow ripple flows along the body,
While all the muscles call to one another:
   "Lift!" and the bulging bale
   Floats like a butterfly in June.

So moved the earliest carrier of bales,
   And the same watchful sun
Glowed through his body feeding it with light.
   So will the last one move,
And halt, and dip his head, and lay his load
Down, and the muscles will relax and tremble. . . .
   Earth, you designed your man
   Beautiful both in labour, and repose.

FIELD EXCURSION

FRIEND, how long have we stood here? The blades of
   grass
Seem growing over our boots, and I hear that tree
Breathing, and under the ground the red worms pass—
And now in the twilight you're suddenly looking at me.

How did all this begin? . . . We adventured a walk
Out of the harbour of home like rudderless ships,
And we lost ourselves, stranded here from the middle of talk,
Gazing into the sky with silent lips.

Waiting for what? Tiptoe on some blade of delight,
Stupid with hope of a beauty we can't understand;
Drowsily caught in the net of approaching night
Held in a torpor of dreams to the pores of the land.

We thought we were grass, or flowers, or dew. We forgot
The murmur of words, and the petulant movement of feet.
We were fortunate free from sound for a time, were we not?
And I hardly know you now that we suddenly meet.

Your hands fall straight to your sides. You are lonely and keen.
I often thought there was something wrong in your ways.
What are you? Where have you come from? What self
    between
You and the you that I know will slip into our days?

But now from the edge of silence I hear you speak:
"Our boots are wet with the heavy dew—and mine leak."
—Let us go home. We have letters to answer. The coal
Is almost out. We've enjoyed our little stroll.

SONG FOR THE MARRIAGE DAY OF A PRINCESS

IT is not well to lavish too much praise
    On those we honour most;
For the loud-speaking or high-sounding phrase
    May seem a boast;
And he does better who with calm voice says:
"I wish you peaceful days."

Poets and rhetoricians make wild speech,
    But five words, ringing true,
May echo clearer and may farther reach
    Than hundreds do.

Therefore let us these five words clearly say:
"We wish you luck to-day."

We English talk quite simply to our friends:
    We tell them all our mind.
Luck we know too: just how it comes, or ends—
    (Strange, hard to find),
So may you please believe us when we say:
We wish you *that* to-day.

And if there's anything, besides, you ask:
    Then we do wish it you.
For us it is no over hardy task
    To speak quite true;
To make an honest proverb, and to say:
We wish you luck to-day.

But, lest there should be anything amiss,
    I add this little phrase:
In the full shine of glory, know you this,
    That, most our praise
Is made of hope, of hope you two may give
Thought to the humble poor that they may live—
Live, and enjoy, like you, and may be sure
That they, like you, rest happy and secure.

FRAGMENT from IT ENDS IN LOVE

I

IF I could catch one stone before it falls
And throw it up and watch where it shall fall,
Or breast the river of almighty blood. . . .

A current can be followed to its source,
I need not swim.
Why should I swim the flood?
I'll walk the bank
Upward, yes upward. . . .
But I know
That something will distract my dreaming steps
And I shall wander from the river-side
Into the meadows of unconscious sleep.

II

Well then I will not try;
I'll come upon the river as by chance
As if an idle walk,
In any country that I might not know,
Had brought me to a stream; and I will say:
"What river can this be?
What do you think? Shall we
Walk for a little up the bank? Not try
To find the source, or watch it flowing by
But move along
Not even listening to its passing song?
Perhaps. . . . Perhaps . . . if thus—"
But no! How, how soon will the one of us
Inevitably with a chance remark
Break up the dream.

III

So I must lie awake, not even sleep,
But study and most carefully pursue
The track of brain to earliest fountain source;
From ancestor to ancestor go back
And mark them one by one

Until at last
I know
Why that continual everlasting flow
Of blood and brain from father passed
From father, and from father, down to son.

IV

Love, you shall take my heart and send
Through generations down, not back,
But forward to the hopeful end
That promise of the aim I lack.
You shall conceive my rambling power,
Take up my body in your blood
And multiply the flowing hour
Through doors to everlasting flood.

HARVEST

WHY does the Earth, oh, work so hard
  To make the crops it loves so well?
And no reward it gets at all
  Though hungry people buy and sell.

We are obliged to think the earth
  Is so impartial and so kind
That no idea of gain or loss
  Has ever lingered in its mind.

Yet in the end we pay in full:
  For after all our toil we give

Our bodies wholly to the earth
And live in it that it may live.

HARBOUR

YOUR quiet and eager eyes wander about,
But, every now and then, return to me,
Contentedly, happily;
And I receive and fold them into mine.
Then my wild heart, though I may look so cool,
Breaks in a shout,
And calls along my body to my brain.
I (O, poor happy fool!)
—I suffer till I find your eyes again:
I want to make your strange eyes always mine.

Now, all your life stay with me! May that look
By which you seek me be my only book.
Your mind is like calm water. I have heard
Words like you, speak in the songs (of some wild bird).
Shall I grow tired of you? I want to die
Before we have to say Good-bye.

Messenger of love, shall we sit here
For ever? And when Time with angry hand
Raps for departure, let us both appear
Lost in our world of love;
We will not move:
We will pretend we do not understand.

No words are needful in the talk we have:
There is more faith in silence than in speech.
But all the little answers I can save
Lie in my heart, and, some time in the night,
They will arise and find their passage right;
And to the middle of your heart will send
Flying arrows of contented love:
We will lie there together, and not move.

ATTEMPTED EXPLANATION

I

I WANTED so to find you. I did wend
  Sprawling through endless glooms, and you did baulk
My explanation; then, my glorious friend,
  I leaned back; rendering foolish all my talk.

That gentle movement of the hand you make;
  That cool known toleration stuns my brain.
For your sweet heart and for your gentle sake
  I leaned to earth, and would not speak again.

II

All that is left of me, since I went round,
  And you were only like yourself, not strained,
As I expected, murmuring no sound
  Of anxious rancour, neither grieved nor pained;

All that is left of me now puts my hat
  Slowly upon my head and goes away,

Humming, and in a minor key and flat:
     "She's had her Say. She has not had her Say.
     Her smile was beautiful, unhappy, gray."

CLOCK

WHEN first you learn to read a clock
That moment you are in a snare,
Doomed for the rest of life to stand
A victim to that patient hand.

The large round eyes of time begin to stare;
The voice of time,
With tick and tock,
Beats like a heart against your ear.

Now all the clocks form close about,
And from the middle of that ring
You crane to find one passage out
In horror what their time may bring.
And is there no escape outside the circle
Where everything you do is overlooked?

I'd like to stare them through the eyes,
And see beyond that moony dial:
For backward from the axis of a clock,
Like gossamer at first,
Tight-braced strands, and cords becoming chains,
Lead, climb, and spread themselves away in space;
So It, their intimate converging place,
Acquires gigantic intricate communions,

Copious relation to forces beyond forces,
(Cool and placid though it look).
Away and away beyond it, range on range,
In all their tortuous elemental courses,
The hidden worlds pursue their time and change;
Are, and then are no more,
Then are again—while we,
Crouched near their ticking dials, faintly guess,
And, as when listening to a far-off ocean,
Hear more, hear less,
Then often not at all,
And visualize the foamy green commotion
Of the great roaring waves that break and fall.

THE BEGGAR

PEACE! There is peace between us.
Listen!
Everyone is tired of you to-night.
We are not the angels you think us.
Don't believe it.
We are men; we only want to be
Natural men to-night, old Mother Beauty.

Take yourself away—
Following and mumbling in our track.
Here's a shilling. Now go home.
Lift your fingers from my shoulder.
Stop it. I have my companions.
They are wondering who you are,

Whispering to me all the time, old woman.
Go. I never knew you.
Leave me. Leave me. Won't you?

LOVE IN THE AUTUMN FOREST

She

LET us go back to London. All the trees
Are dying in the forest.

He

Though you fear death.
I thought you would like the colour of the leaves.

She

Let us not remember autumn forests.
Let us forget this falling of the leaves.
In London nothing dies among the streets.

And you will not love me for ever—it is not true.
Say nothing here that is not wholly true;
Or we may hate each other.

Why did we leave the shining pavement;
Pass away from the roaring road?
In London we are known to each other.
But here
Our vows fall like dead leaves.

He

You have slipped your tether.
There, I could well believe you loved the trees;
But here, I see you hate them by your eyes.

Mist clings in your hair.
You stand like a strange martyr.
It hurts you to remain so still.
The leaves are falling in the wood; they are falling;
And life is dumb. We will return.

There, in London we will laugh again.
The tame trees in the square will be enough.
We need not see their leaves fall at our feet.

She

Oh, the autumnal horror covers me.
I wish I could be buried in the leaves.

THIS OUR LIFE

I HAD the invitation of the King
To go into his House, and, innocent
(Young as I was), I let his servants bring,
And helplessly received, the gifts he sent.
These were they: feet, hands, eyes and right-of-birth;
The clothing and condition of a man;
The strange and ancient liberty of earth.
These I must hold, and use them as I can.

Feet bring fatigue; hands, pain; eyes, too much sight;
Birth, rapture, that declines in doubt and sighing:
The vaunted, vast, and everlasting right
Of living is the liberty of dying.
  "O Lord, have you no other gifts?" I call.
  But he moves silently about his Hall.

EVENING

NOW the cool twilight, glowing,
Falls like dew
Upon the city's brow.
Now fretful day is slowing;
Slowly the river flows, but men are going
Swiftly, as though they knew
At last some hope beyond all silence. Now
To us who wait it seems we had to climb
For this one evening up the hill of Time.

We wait. We wait.
Surely the wings that hold,
Dark-clasped, the mystery of Fate
This moment will unfold.

Now the great hand is lifted that will strike
The final crash on doubt;
The rosy clouds are parted like
Lips that blow some candle out.
The deep breath of the moment is indrawn,
Holds, with wide nostrils, back the final call.
We smile because we know ere dawn

Silence in heavy dust, shall fall.
To-morrow evening all this past will seem
A drifted ancient dream.

Now all the veins of Time are running cool.
Night lies before us like a silent pool.
Oh, at this final moment it is sweet
To go home swiftly through the lighted street.

DEDICATION

CHILD of the Earth, shall we walk?
Your hands have been busy so long to-day.
Are you tired? Let us go to the meadow-pool.
Out on the grass it is cool;
Cool in the song of the nightingale;
Cool in the meadow. The moon is cool.

STRANGE MEETINGS

I

IF suddenly a clod of earth should rise,
And walk about, and breathe, and speak, and love,
How one would tremble, and in what surprise
    Gasp: "Can *you* move?"

I see men walking, and I always feel:
"Earth! How have you done this? What can you be?"

I can't learn how to know men, or conceal
How strange they are to me.

II

The dark space underneath is full of bones,
The surface filled with bodies—roving men,
And floating above the surface a foam of eyes:
Over that is Heaven. All the Gods
Walk with cool feet, paddle among the eyes;
Scatter them like foam-flakes on the wind
Over the human world.

III

Rising toward the surface, we are men
A moment, till we dive again, and then
We take our ease of breathing: we are sent
Unconscious to our former element,
There being perfect, living without pain
Till we emerge like men, and meet again.

IV

You live there; I live here:
Other people everywhere
Haunt their houses, and endure
Days and deeds and furniture,
Circumstances, families,
And the stare of foreign eyes.

V

Often we must entertain,
Tolerantly if we can,

Ancestors returned again
Trying to be modern man.
Gates of Memory are wide;
All of them can shuffle in,
Join the family, and, once inside,
Alas, what a disturbance they begin!
Creatures of another time and mood,
They wrangle; they dictate;
Bawl their experience into brain and blood,
Call themselves *Fate*.

VI

Eyes float above the surface, trailing
Obedient bodies, lagging feet.
Where the wind of words is wailing
Eyes and voices part and meet.

VII

BIRTH

One night when I was in the House of Death,
A shrill voice penetrated root and stone,
And the whole earth was shaken under ground:
I woke and there was light above my head.

Before I heard that shriek I had not known
The region of Above from Underneath,
Alternate light and dark, silence and sound,
Difference between the living and the dead.

VIII

It is difficult to tell
(Though we feel it well),
How the surface of the land

Budded into head and hand:
But it is a great surprise
How it blossomed into eyes.

IX

A flower is looking through the ground,
Blinking at the April weather;
Now a child has seen the flower:
Now they go and play together.

Now it seems the flower will speak,
And will call the child its brother—
But, oh strange forgetfulness!—
They don't recognise each other.

X

Yesterday I heard a thrush;
He held me with his eyes:
I waited on my yard of earth,
He watched me from his skies.

My whole day was penetrated
By his wild and windy cries,
And the glitter of his eyes.

XI

The stars must make an awful noise
In whirling round the sky;
Yet somehow I can't even hear
Their loudest song or sigh.

So it is wonderful to think
One blackbird can outsing
The voice of all the swarming stars
On any day in spring.

XII

Oh, how reluctantly some people learn
To hold their bones together, with what toil
Breathe and are moved, as though they would return,
How gladly, and be crumbled into soil!

They knock their groping bodies on the stones,
Blink at the light, and startle at all sound,
With their white lips learn only a few moans,
Then go back under ground.

XIII

The ploughboy, he could never understand—
While he was carried dozing in the cart,
Or strolling with the plough across the land,
He never knew he had a separate heart.

Had someone told him, had he understood,
It would have been like tearing up the ground.
He slowly moves and slowly grows like wood,
And does not turn his head for any sound.

So they mistook him for a clod of land,
And round him, while he dreamed, they built a town.
He rubs his eyes; he cannot understand,
But like a captive wanders up and down.

112

XIV

You may not ever go to heaven;
You had better love the earth:
You'll achieve, for all your pain,
(What you cannot understand)
Privilege to drive a flower
Through an inch of land.
All the world is in your brain:
Worship it, in human power,
With your body and your hand.

XV

I often stood at my open gate,
  Watching the passing crowd with no surprise:
I don't think I had used my eyes for hate
  Till they met your eyes.

I don't believe this road is meant for you,
  Or, if it be,
Will no one say what I am meant to do
  Now while you stare at me?

XVI

How did you enter that body? Why are you here?
At once, when I had seen your eyes appear
Over the brim of earth, they were looking for me.
How suddenly, how silently
We rose into this long-appointed place.
From what sleep have you arrived,
That your beauty has survived?
You, the everlasting—you
Known before a word was. . . .

XVII

To-day, when you were sitting in the house,
And I was walking to you from the town,
At the far corner of the alder-wood,
I'm certain you were strolling up and down.

I thought: "She's come to meet me, and meanwhile
Is talking to the cowslips in the dew."
Just as you saw me, and began to smile—
It was not you.

Now I'm not certain—for how shall I say?
I cannot tell, however I may stare,
If it be you here in the house all day,
Or whether you are wandering still out there.

XVIII

Wipe away, please,
That film from your eyes.
I can't see you plainly. Are you
The friend that I seem to remember? Are we
The people I think we must be?
We have talked for an hour: it seems you are he.
I know you, I'm sure, though your eyes are so altered.
Oh, in what life of our lives did we meet?—
But you smile, then you sigh, then you frown:
Now you stare at me angrily. How can it be?
I know you—you do not know me.

XIX

A man who has clung to a branch and he hangs—
  Wondering when it will break.

A woman who sits by the bed of a child,
    Watching for him to wake.

People who gaze at the town-hall clock,
    Waiting to hear the hour.

Somebody walking along a path,
    Stooping to pick a flower.

Dawn; and the reaper comes out of his home,
    Moving along to mow.

A frightened crowd in a little room,
    Waiting all day to go.

A tall man rubbing his eyes in the dusk,
    Muttering "Yes"; murmuring "No."

xx

It is not difficult to die:
You hold your breath and go to sleep;
Your skin turns white or grey or blue,
And some of your relations weep.

The cheerful clock without a pause
Will finish your suspended day.
That body you were building up
Will suddenly be thrown away.

You turn your fingers to the ground,
Drop all the things you had to do:
It is the first time in your life
You'll cease completely to be you.

Memory opens; memory closes:
Memory taught me to be a man.

It remembers everything:
It helps the little birds to sing.

It finds the honey for the bee:
It opens and closes, opens and closes. . . .

> —*Proverbs for the humble wise;*
> *Flashes out of human eyes;*
> *Oracles of paradise.*

JOURNEY

I

HOW many times I nearly miss the train
By running up the staircase once again
For some dear trifle almost left behind.
At that last moment the unwary mind
Forgets the solemn tick of station-time;
That muddy lane the feet must climb—
The bridge—the ticket—signal down—
Train just emerging beyond the town:
The great blue engine panting as it takes
The final curve, and grinding on its brakes
Up to the platform-edge. . . . The little doors
Swing open, while the burly porter roars.
The tight compartment fills: our careful eyes

Go to explore each others' destinies.
A lull. The station-master waves. The train
Gathers, and grips, and takes the rails again,
Moves to the shining open land, and soon
Begins to tittle-tattle a tame tattoon.

II

They ramble through the country-side,
Dear gentle monsters, and we ride
Pleasantly seated—so we sink
Into a torpor on the brink
Of thought, or read our books, and understand
Half them and half the backward-gliding land:
(Trees in a dance all twirling round;
Large rivers flowing with no sound;
The scattered images of town and field,
Shining flowers half concealed.)
And, having settled to an equal rate,
They swing the curve and straighten to the straight,
Curtail their stride and gather up their joints,
Snort, dwindle their steam for the noisy points,
Leap them in safety, and, the other side,
Loop again to an even stride.

The long train moves: we move in it along.
Like an old ballad, or an endless song,
It drones and wimbles its unwearied croon—
Croons, drones, and mumbles all the afternoon.

Towns with their fifty chimneys close and high,
Wreathed in great smoke between the earth and sky,
It hurtles through them, and you think it must

Halt—but it shrieks and sputters them with dust,
Cracks like a bullet through their big affairs,
Rushes the station-bridge, and disappears
Out to the suburb, laying bare
Each garden trimmed with pitiful care;
Children are caught at idle play,
Held a moment, and thrown away.
Nearly everyone looks round.
Some dignified inhabitant is found
Right in the middle of the commonplace—
Buttoning his trousers, or washing his face.

III

Oh the wild engine! Every time I sit
In any train I must remember it.
The way it smashes through the air; its great
Petulant majesty and terrible rate:
Driving the ground before it, with those round
Feet pounding, beating, covering the ground;
The piston using up the white steam so
You cannot watch it when it come or go;
The cutting, the embankment; how it takes
The tunnels, and the clatter that it makes;
So careful of the train and of the track,
Guiding us out, or helping us go back;
Breasting its destination: at the close
Yawning, and slowly dropping to a doze.

IV

We who have looked each other in the eyes
This journey long, and trundled with the train,

Now to our separate purposes must rise,
Becoming decent strangers once again.
The little chamber we have made our home
In which we so conveniently abode,
The complicated journey we have come,
Must be an unremembered episode.
Our common purpose made us all like friends.
How suddenly it ends!
A nod, a murmur, or a little smile,
Or often nothing, and away we file.

I hate to leave you, comrades. I will stay
To watch you drift apart and pass away.
It seems impossible to go and meet
All those strange eyes of people in the street.
But, like some proud unconscious god, the train
Gathers us up and scatters us again.

EVERY THING

SINCE man has been articulate,
Mechanical, improvidently wise,
(Servant of Fate),
He has not understood the little cries
And foreign conversations of the small
Delightful creatures that have followed him
Not far behind;
Has failed to hear the sympathetic call
Of Crockery and Cutlery, those kind
Reposeful Teraphim

Of his domestic happiness; the Stool
He sat on, or the Door he entered through:
He has not thanked them, overbearing fool!
What is he coming to?

But you should listen to the talk of these.
Honest they are, and patient they have kept,
Served him without his *Thank-you* or his *Please*. . . .
I often heard
The gentle Bed, a sigh between each word,
Murmuring, before I slept.
The Candle, as I blew it, cried aloud,
Then bowed,
And in a smoky argument
Into the darkness went.
The Kettle puffed a tentacle of breath :—
"Pooh! I have boiled his water, I don't know
Why; and he always says I boil too slow.
He never calls me 'Sukie dear,' and oh,
I wonder why I squander my desire
Sitting submissive on his kitchen fire."

Now the old Copper Basin suddenly
Rattled and tumbled from the shelf,
Bumping and crying: "I can fall by myself;
Without a woman's hand
To patronise and coax and flatter me,
I understand
The lean and poise of gravitable land."
It gave a raucous and tumultuous shout,
Twisted itself convulsively about,
Rested upon the floor, and, while I stare,
It stares and grins at me.
The old impetuous Gas above my head

Begins irascibly to flare and fret,
Wheezing into its epileptic jet,
Reminding me I ought to go to bed.

The Rafters creak; an Empty-Cupboard door
Swings open; now a wild Plank of the floor
Breaks from its joist, and leaps behind my foot.
Down from the chimney half a pound of Soot
Tumbles, and lies, and shakes itself again.
The Putty cracks against the window-pane.
A piece of Paper in the basket shoves
Another piece, and toward the bottom moves.
My independent Pencil, while I write,
Breaks at the point: the ruminating Clock
Stirs all its body and begins to rock,
Warning the waiting presence of the Night,
Strikes the dead hour, and tumbles to the plain
Ticking of ordinary work again.

You do well to remind me, and I praise
Your strangely individual foreign ways.
You call me from myself to recognise
Companionship in your unselfish eyes.
I want your dear acquaintances, although
I pass you arrogantly over, throw
Your lovely sounds, and squander them along
My busy days. I'll do you no more wrong.
Purr for me, Sukie, like a faithful cat.
You, my well trampled Boots, and you, my Hat,
Remain my friends: I feel, though I don't speak,
Your touch grow kindlier from week to week.
It well becomes our mutual happiness
To go toward the same end more or less.
There is not much dissimilarity,

Not much to choose, I know it well, in fine,
Between the purposes of you and me,
And your eventual Rubbish Heap, and mine.

CORONILLA

I

CORONILLA! Coronilla!
  Heavy yellow tepid bloom:
(Midnight in a scented room)—
  Coronilla.

Southern road; muffled house . . .
  Later on to-night
I'll come again so quietly
  By moonlight.

.   .   .   .   .

Oh, what is that I think I see
  So pale beyond the yellow dusk,
Beyond the trailing bitter flower
  And reek of marrow-bone and musk?

Is it a face?—My frozen hands
  Are hiding in their bone:
The stare above the little mouth;
  And she and I alone.

She calls me. Oh, I wonder why.
  She wants me. Shall I go?
Now is your time, my brain, to cry
  The often-practised *No*.

Conorilla, I have passed you
    Seven times a day.
Why do I always take my walk
    The southern way?

Although I hate your bitter reek,
    I still return, and still
Long that your hidden voice may speak
    Against my wavering will.

Wait for me. I will come to-morrow.
    Must you have your way?
Wait, then; I will come to-morrow.
    I am going home to-day.

    .   .   .   .   .

Coronilla! Coronilla!
    Are you here to-night?
Seven times I've come to you
    By moonlight.

Now I must feel your tepid bloom.
    I'll twist your tendrils through my skin;
So, if you have a shuttered room,
    Coronilla, let me in.

II

He cooled the hollow of his cheek,
    And filled it with the drowsy flower.
He has become so gentle, weak,
    And feverish in her power.

123

Now all the sappy little leaves
　　Are clinging to his frozen lips;
And she has drawn the shutter back,
　　And drawn him with her finger-tips.

The candles flicker in the room.
　　He trembles by the wall.
She gave him all and all again,
　　But still he asks for all.

So one by one the candles droop
　　And close their eyes and faint away.
The yellow blooms begin to stoop:
　　He has not noticed it is day.

III

Now he has laid his body down,
　　And all his skin is silver pale;
He'll never, never rise again:
　　His muscles have begun to fail.

He's covered with a winding sheet.
　　There's yet a little time to rave,
Then he will hear the grains of earth
　　Drip-dropping on his grave.

Yellow, yellow is the flower;
　　Fatal is the bloom;
And no one any time returned
　　Who slept inside the shuttered room.

WEEK-END

THE train! The twelve o'clock for paradise.
  Hurry, or it will try to creep away.
Out in the country everyone is wise:
  We can be only wise on Saturday.
There you are waiting, little friendly house:
  Those are your chimney-stacks with you between,
Surrounded by old trees and strolling cows,
  Staring through all your windows at the green.
Your homely floor is creaking for our tread;
  The smiling teapot with contented spout
Thinks of the boiling water, and the bread
  Longs for the butter. All their hands are out
    To greet us, and the gentle blankets seem
    Purring and crooning: "Lie in us, and dream."

II

The key will stammer, and the door reply,
  The hall wake, yawn, and smile; the torpid stair
Will grumble at our feet, the table cry:
  "Fetch my belongings for me; I am bare."
A clatter! Something in the attic falls.
  A ghost has lifted up his robes and fled.
The loitering shadows move along the walls;
  Then silence very slowly lifts his head.
The starling with impatient screech has flown
  The chimney, and is watching from the tree.
They thought us gone for ever: mouse alone
  Stops in the middle of the floor to see.
    Now all you idle things, resume your toil.
    Hearth, put your flames on. Sulky kettle, boil.

III

Contented evening; comfortable joys;
    The snoozing fire, and all the fields are still:
Tranquil delight, no purpose, and no noise—
    Unless the slow wind flowing round the hill.
"Murry" (the kettle) dozes; little mouse
    Is rambling prudently about the floor.
There's lovely conversation in this house:
    Words become princes that were slaves before.
What a sweet atmosphere for you and me
    The people that have been here left behind. . . .
Oh, but I fear it may turn out to be
    Built of a dream, erected in the mind:
        So if we speak too loud, we may awaken
        To find it vanished, and ourselves mistaken.

IV

Lift up the curtain carefully. All the trees
    Stand in the dark like drowsy sentinels.
The oak is talkative to-night; he tells
    The little bushes crowding at his knees
That formidable, hard, voluminous
    History of growth from acorn into age.
They titter like school-children; they arouse
    Their comrades, who exclaim: "He is very sage."
Look how the moon is staring through that cloud,
    Laying and lifting idle streaks of light.
O, hark! was that the monstrous wind, so loud
    And sudden, prowling always through the night?
        Let down the shaking curtain. They are queer,
        Those foreigners. They and we live so near.

V

Come, come to bed. The shadows move about,
  And someone seems to overhear our talk.
The fire is low; the candles flicker out;
  The ghosts of former tenants want to walk.
Already they are shuffling through the gloom.
  I felt an old man touch my shoulder-blade;
Once he was married here: they love this room,
  He and his woman and the child they made.
Dead, dead, they are, yet some familiar sound,
  Creeping along the brink of happy life,
Revives their memory from under ground—
  The farmer and his troublesome old wife.
      Let us be going: as we climb the stairs,
      They'll sit down in our warm half-empty chairs.

VI

Morning! Wake up! Awaken! All the boughs
  Are rippling on the air across the green.
The youngest birds are singing to the house.
  Blood of the world!—and is the country clean?
Disturb the precinct. Cool it with a shout.
  Sing as you trundle down to light the fire.
Turn the encumbering shadows tumbling out,
  And fill the chambers with a new desire.
Life is no good, unless the morning brings
  White happiness and quick delight of day.
These half-inanimate domestic things
  Must all be useful, or must go away.
      Coffee, be fragrant. Porridge in my plate,
      Increase the vigour to fulfil my fate.

VII

The fresh air moves like water round a boat.
    The white clouds wander. Let us wander too.
The whining wavering plover flap and float.
    That crow is flying after that cuckoo.
Look! Look! . . . They're gone. What are the great trees
    calling?
Just come a little farther, by that edge
Of green, to where the stormy ploughland, falling
    Wave upon wave, is lapping to the hedge.
Oh, what a lovely bank! Give me your hand.
    Lie down and press your heart against the ground.
Let us both listen till we understand,
    Each through the other, every natural sound. . . .

        I can't hear anything to-day, can you,
        But, far and near: "Cuckoo! Cuckoo! Cuckoo!"?

VIII

The everlasting grass—how bright, how cool!
    The day has gone too suddenly, too soon.
There's something white and shiny in that pool—
    Throw in a stone, and you will hit the moon.
Listen, the church-bell ringing! Do not say
    We must go back to-morrow to our work.
We'll tell them we are dead: we died to-day.
    We're lazy. We're too happy. We will shirk.
We're cows. We're kettles. We'll be anything
    Except the manikins of time and fear.
We'll start away to-morrow wandering,
    And nobody will notice in a year. . . .
        Now the great sun is slipping under ground.
        Grip firmly!—How the earth is whirling round.

128

IX

Be staid; be careful; and be not too free.
Temptation to enjoy your liberty
May rise against you, break into a crime,
And smash the habit of employing Time.
It serves no purpose that the careful clock
  Mark the appointment, the officious train
Hurry to keep it, if the minutes mock
  Loud in your ear: "Late. Late. Late. Late again."
Week-end is very well on Saturday:
  On Monday it's a different affair—
A little episode, a trivial stay
  In some oblivious spot somehow, somewhere.
      On Sunday night we hardly laugh or speak:
      Week-end begins to merge itself in Week.

X

Pack up the house, and close the creaking door.
  The fields are dull this morning in the rain.
It's difficult to leave that homely floor.
  Wave a light hand; we will return again.
(What was that bird?) Good-bye, ecstatic tree,
  Floating, bursting, and breathing on the air.
The lonely farm is wondering that we
  Can leave. How every window seems to stare!
That bag is heavy. Share it for a bit.
  You like that gentle swashing of the ground
As we tread? . . .
               It is over. Now we sit
  Reading the morning paper in the sound
      Of the debilitating heavy train.
      London again, again. London again.

ASPIDISTRA STREET

GO along that road, and look at sorrow.
Every window grumbles.
All day long the drizzle fills the puddles,
Trickles in the runnels and the gutters,
Drips and drops and dripples, drops and dribbles,
While the melancholy aspidistra
Frowns between the parlour curtains.

Uniformity, dull Master!—
Birth and marriage, middle-age and death;
Rain and gossip: Sunday, Monday, Tuesday . . .

Sure, the lovely fools who made Utopia
Planned it without any aspidistra.
There will be a heaven on earth, but first
We must banish from the parlour
Plush and poker-work and paper flowers,
Brackets, staring photographs and what-nots,
Serviettes, frills and etageres,
Anti-macassars, vases, chiffonniers;

And the gloomy aspidistra
Glowering through the window-pane,
Meditating heavy maxims,
Moralising to the rain.

THE FOUNDERED TRAM

THERE it lies:—
An injured toad,

Tumbled away to the side of the road,
Dashed from the track of its shiny slime;
Silly sight for pausing eyes:
Skeptic of the rules of Time . . .
Where has it thrown its respectable load?

Passive inhabitants—how they were hurled
Into a sudden other world;

Jagged fragments of glass lie down
Each like a frozen cry or frown.

Oh what a change! And what a strange
Upheaval of hands must have gone to that,
Or following plunge at a falling hat,
Or lurching into a broken thigh,
All to the spurt of one question: *Why?*

That heavy load of metal found
An easy lean, and sharply went
Over to attractive ground,
Better to lie down content
(Better than the captive glide)
Lazily upon its side—
Element to element.

CAT'S MEAT

HO, all you cats in all the street;
Look out, it is the hour of meat:

The little barrow is crawling along,
And the meat-boy growling his fleshy song.

Hurry, Ginger! Hurry, White!
Don't delay to court or fight.

Wandering Tabby, vagrant Black,
Yamble from adventure back!

Slip across the shining street,
Meat! Meat! Meat! Meat!

Lift your tail and dip your feet;
Find your penny—Meat! Meat!

Where's your mistress? Learn to purr:
Pennies emanate from her.

Be to her, for she is Fate,
Perfectly affectionate.

(You, domestic Pinkie-Nose,
Keep inside and warm your toes.)

Flurry, flurry in the street—
Meat! Meat! Meat! Meat!

BLACKBERRY

HEDGE is like a breaking wave;
Thorns are stinging like the sea.—
Lean tiptoe, or plunge, to pick
Sparkling clustered blackberry.

Savage little eyes they keep
Blinking through their juicy spray.
Every-hidden-where they peep,
Tantalising us all day.

Oh, a wild and dusky store,
Plentiful and free to all:
We will keep a Blackberry Feast—
Bramble-jelly-festival.

Boys with baskets empty-full,
Girls, with happy laughter, singing,
Wander everywhere to pull.
Small sweet children call and run
And prick their little fingers; autumn sun
Glitters over everyone.

Everybody will be bringing
Fragrant loads by field and hill
Homeward into Blackberry Mill.

CHANGE OF MIND

HOW the rain tumbles. Lord!—
Only last week I would have gone all night
Dripping and scurrying, of my own accord,
For just one sight
Of you. How can I be so bored
Now at your short imploring note?

I curse the ugly rain and you.
I know exactly how you wrote,
Smiling—and sobbing too. . . .
I will stay here. I will not go to you.

I know precisely how you'll look;
I can imagine every word you'll say;
I want to close you like a finished book:
Please let me have my way.

Why must I tell you that our love is done?
It lasted well, but now you have begun
To sorrow me. Be wise and understand.
Whatever purpose can be served indeed
By going two enormous rainy miles
To hold your hand?
Or is there any need
To trudge the lane, and climb the slippery stiles,
When, by this fire, and snugly in my brain,
I, without effort, may
Press your dry lips and hold your hands again,
And answer every word you'll have to say?

But I'm forgetting something. . . . Who was that
Loafing about your cottage all last week?
How cool he was, and always sat
Watching you, and would not speak.
Why was he there; and is he still?
It's raining less, I think. Who can he be?
Shall I put on my coat? I think I will.
He may—may not, be gone. I'll go and see.
I'll go and find out why you sent for me.

WINTER MILK

THE cows are in the long byre, low, half-dark.
Now that it is twilight, let us roam
Past the white farm where the dog must bark,
Over mud to fetch milk home.

The byre is like a church, dim, melancholy,
With low windows gleaming like painted glass.
Over uneven brickways slowly,
Watched by the solemn black cow, we pass.

Her horns gleam; her tall haunches slope and fall
Curving to her neck; her lazy limbs
Droop, and she chews, while her halter swings.
That large man far away by the end wall
Is milking the white cow: all the time he sings,
Esoteric canticles and farmyard hymns.

Half-a-dozen boys and girls, laughing together,
Lean on the barn-wall waiting for milk.
The hawthorn-bearded ploughman is grumbling at the
      weather.
The milk is softly falling with a sound like moving silk.

Gloomy philosophers; great grim cows,
Chewing and ruminating all in a row:
Wise stupid creatures with haughty brows,
What kind of thing are they pretending to know?

.   .   .   .   .

Now the sound of pouring droops, fails.
There's a clatter of pails,

A movement of haunches, a rolling of eyes.
Some of the cows doze; some of them rise.

A joke is cracked: everybody smiles.
We pay for our milk; we take our little can;
We murmur good-night to the pink-faced man:
We wander through evening home quiet two miles.

TREES

I

ONE summer afternoon, you find
Some lonely trees. Persuade your mind
To drowse. Then, as your eyelids close,
And you still hover into those
Three stages of a darkening doze,
This side the barrier of sleep,
Pause. In that last clear moment open quick
Your sight toward where the green is bright and thick.
Be sure that everything you keep
To dream with is made out of trees.
Grip hard, become a root, so drive
Your muscles through the ground alive
That you'll be breaking from above your knees
Out into branches. Let your manhood be
Forgotten, your whole purpose seem
The purpose of a simple tree
Rooted in a quiet dream.

I did that. It is difficult to cease
Thinking. A thought will rise and trip
Your spirit on the brink of peace,

So your tough muscles lose their grip.
It will be hard to find
A way to lead you out of Mind,
And after that to keep
The passage of a natural sleep.

(Any silly man can swim
Down the channel of a dream,
Dawdling under banks of green.
That's an easy drift for him,
Snoozing like a little stream,
And a comfortable whim
Any shallow man can dream.
Water is a lazy thing,
Lipping at an edge of ground,
Elbowing and muttering.
I have heard a little stream
Imitate a human dream.)

The trees throw up their singing leaves, and climb
Spray over spray. They break through Time.
Their roots lash through the clay. They lave
The earth, and wash along the ground;
They burst in green wave over wave,
Fly in a blossom of light foam;
Rank following windy rank they come:
They flood the plain,
Swill through the valley, top the mound,
Flow over the low hill,
Curl round
The bases of the mountains, fill
Their crevices, and stain
Their ridges green. . . . Be sure you keep
Some memory of this for sleep.

Then hold your blood, contrive to fill
Your veins with sap. Now dive; now sink
Below the spray. Relax your will. . . .
The earth still has you by the heel?
(Do not remember what you feel!) . . .
Lift up your head above the spray.
Pull (so trees live). Thrust! Drive your way!
The agony of One Idea will twist
Your branches. (Can you feel the dew?)
The wind will cuff you with his fist.
The birds will build their nests in you.
Your circulating blood will go
Flowing five hundred times more slow.
A thousand veils will darkly press
About your muffled consciousness:
So will you grow;
You will not know,
Not wonder, why you grow. . . .

II

I was cast up from that still tide of sleep,
I suddenly awakened—could not keep
A tranquil growth.
I heard the swinging clocks of man:
And I was conscious of unworthy sloth.
Oh, silly tree-adept!—
Out of arboreal delight I crept;
Crept, was afraid, and ran—
Too much mortality I kept.

They drove me forth. The angry trees
Roared till I tumbled lean and lewd
Out of their Paradise. The forest rose

To scourge my wavering conscience, and pursued.
A thousand doors clapped roughly and were close.
Low growling voices on that other side
Cursed in a tone of old offended wood. . . .

III

It is a dangerous journey. If you go
Think carefully of this, which now I know.—
Tree-growth is but a corridor between
The Seen and the Unseen.
Trees are like sentinels that keep
The passage of a gate
From this sleep to that other sleep:
Between two worlds they wait.
If they discover you, you cannot hide.
Run backward. They are stern.
You may be driven out that other side,
And not return.

Better perhaps you love them distantly—
So if they tempt you, as a woman might,
Make of their love an Immorality;
And if they haunt you, regulate your sight
That tree-love may seem like Adultery;
And never visit them at all by night.
Lock door, draw curtains, close yourself within
When the cool flow of sunset shall begin:
Leave them to float alone about their gold.
But when the moon comes to them and they fold
Dark branches round her, you'll be jealous then—
Focus your vision and contract it near:
Read some new book, talk leisurely with men.
Banish their nightingales, and yet I fear

How they may call and echo through your sleep. . . .
There will be many sounds you must not hear
If you would keep
The ways of manly wisdom, and not be
Distracted by the love of any tree.

There are some men, of course, some men, I know,
Who, when they pass,
Seem like trees walking, and to grow
From earth, and, native in the grass,
(So taut their muscles) move on gliding roots.
They blossom every day: their fruits
Are always new and cover the happy ground.
Wherever they may stand
You hear inevitable sound
Of birds and branches, harvest and all delights
Of pastured and wooded land.
For them it is not dangerous to go
Each side that barrier moving to and fro:
They without trepidation undertake
Excursions into sleep, and safely come awake.

But it is different, different for me,
(Also for you I fear)
To whom a tree seems something more than tree,
And when we see,
Clustered together, two or three,
We almost are afraid to pass them near.
How beautifully they grow,
Above their stiles and lanes and watery places,
Crowding the brink of silence everywhere,
With branches dipping low.
To smile toward us or to stroke our faces.
They drown us in their summer, and swirl round,

Leaving us faint: so nobody is free,
But always some surrounding ground
Is swamped and washed and covered in by tree.

They follow us and haunt us. We must build
Houses of wood. Our evening rooms are filled
With fragments of the forest: chairs and tables.
We swing our wooden doors;
Pile up, divide our sheds, byres, stables
With logs, make wooden stairs, lay wooden floors,
Sit, move, and sleep among the limbs of trees,
Rejoicing to be near them. How men saw,
Chisel and hammer, carve and tease
All timber to their purpose, modelling
The forest in their chambers. And the raw
Wild stuff, built like a cupboard or a shelf,
Will crack and shiver in the night, and sing,
Reminding everybody of itself;
Out of decayed old centuries will bring
A sudden memory
Of growing tree.

IV

And they are felled. The hatchet swings:
They pass their way. . . . Some learn to sail
Seaward on white enormous wings,
Scattering blossom along their trail;
Or be a little ship that ploughs
And glides across the rippled land,
Great frothing steeds high mounted at the bows,
Calm at the helm the ploughboy's guiding hand,
Crowded with sailing birds that flap and float,
Hang stiff against the air and hold the breeze,

Landworthy, and as trim a boat
As ever ploughed the seas.

So they are felled. . . . They change, they come,
Lingering their period of decay
In transitory forms; and some
Lie Sleeping all that shining Way
The lanky greyhound engines loop,
With open nostrils flashing by,
Lugging their drowsy noisy troupe—
They clank and clatter, crouch and cry,
Pass, vanish, fill the distance with a sigh.
And some, some trees, before they die,
Carved and moulded small,
Suddenly begin,
Oh, what a wild and windy woodland call
Out of the lips of the violin!

So trees are felled. . . . But Tree
Lingers immovably where it has stood,
Living its tranquil immortality
Impassive to the death of wood.

And you—be certain that you keep
Some memory of trees for sleep.

LAMENT IN 1915 (*B. H. W.*)

I CALL you, and I call you. Oh come home,
You lonely creature. Curse the foreign clown
Who plugged you with that lead, and knocked you down.

Stand up again and laugh, you wandering friend;
Say, as you would: "It's just a little hole;
It will soon mend."
Walk now into the room. Come! Come! Come! Come!

Come! we will laugh together all the night.
(We shall have poured ourselves a glass or two.)
Sit down. Our mutual mirth will reach its height
When we remember how they called you dead,
And I shall ask you how it felt, and you—
"Oh, nothing. Just a tumble. Rather hot,
The feeling in my side; and then my head
A trifle dizzy, but I'm back again.
I lay out there too long, and I've still got,
When I think of it, just a little pain."

I know the way you tumbled. . . . Once you slid
And landed on your side. I noticed then
A trick of falling; some peculiar glide—
A curious movement, not like other men.
But did your mouth drop open? Did your breath
Hurt you? What sort of feeling quickly came,
When you discovered that it might be death?

And what will happen if I shout your name?
Perhaps you may be there behind the door,
And if I raise my voice a little more,
You'll swing it open. I don't know how thick
The black partition is between us two.
Answer, if you can hear me; friend, be quick. . . .
Listen, the door-bell rang! Perhaps it's you.

You're in the room. You're sitting in that chair.
You are! . . . I will go down. It *was* the bell.
You *may* be waiting at the door as well.

Am I not certain I shall find you there ? . . .

You're rigged in your best uniform to-day;
You take a momentary martial stand,
Then step inside and hold me out your hand,
And laugh in that old solitary way.

You don't know why you did it. All this while
You've slaved and sweated. Now you're very strong,
And so you tell me with a knowing smile:
"We're going out to Flanders before long."
I thought you would come back with an ugly hole
Below your thigh,
And ask for sympathy and wander lame;
I thought you'ld be that same
Grumbling companion without self-control—
I never thought you'ld die.

.   .   .   .   .

Now let us both forget this brief affair:
Let us begin our friendship all again.
I'm going down to meet you on the stair.
Walk to me! Come! for I can see you plain.
How strange! A moment I did think you dead.
How foolish of me!
Friend! friend! Are you dumb?
Why are you pale? Why do you hang your head?
You see me? Here's my hand. Why don't you come?
Don't make me angry. You are there, I know.
Is not my house your house? There is a bed
Upstairs. You're tired. Lie down; you must come home.
Some men are killed . . . not you. Be as you were.

And yet—Somehow it's dark down all the stair.
I'm standing at the door. You are not there.

THE BIRD AT DAWN

WHAT I saw was just one eye
In the dawn as I was going:
A bird can carry all the sky
In that little button glowing.

Never in my life I went
So deep into a firmament.

He was standing on a tree,
All in blossom overflowing;
And purposely looked hard at me,
At first, as if to question merrily:
"Where are you going?"
But next some far more serious thing to say:
I could not answer, could not look away.

Oh, that hard, round, and so distracting eye:
Little mirror of all sky!—
And then the after-song another tree
Held, and sent radiating back on me.

If no man had invented human word,
And a bird-song had been
The only way to utter what we mean,
What would we men have heard,

What understood, what seen,
Between the trills and pauses, in between
The singing and the silence of a bird?

SOLITUDE

WHEN you have tidied all things for the night,
And while your thoughts are fading to their sleep,
You'll pause a moment in the late firelight,
Too sorrowful to weep.

The large and gentle furniture has stood
In sympathetic silence all the day
With that old kindness of domestic wood;
Nevertheless the haunted room will say:
"Some one must be away."

The little dog rolls over half awake,
Stretches his paws, yawns, looking up at you,
Wags his tail very slightly for your sake,
That you may feel he is unhappy too.

A distant engine whistles, or the floor
Creaks, or the wandering night-wind bangs a door.

Silence is scattered like a broken glass.
The minutes prick their ears and run about,
Then one by one subside again and pass
Sedately in, monotonously out.

You bend your head and wipe away a tear.
Solitude walks one heavy step more near.

INVITATION TO A SEA-HOLIDAY

F ROM hopeless London we can find a way,
Surely, to daylight and the biting spray?
Trains there will be that go
We know
Rasping along their rails at gorgeous rate.
Come then, my comrade, O delightful mate,
And let us find
That cliff where rough invigorating wind
Shall blow salt air into our London faces,
For there are many places.

What then? We shall be like two specks of dust
Brushed out of London. Soon our tarnished eyes
Shaking away their rust
Will take the lively light of clean surprise.

We shall go swinging down some railway line,
Glancing on green small fields with casual eye;
Thinking (and only that) of shoring brine.
Perhaps our bodies peacefully may lie
On sand while ocean at its gentle rate
Shoreward, may be our own to contemplate.

We shall be humming as we go along
Singing, indeed, within our tired brains
The sea's anticipated song
Which the glad holiday at length attains.

Look how all people rush toward the sea,
Knowing perhaps their origin so old;
Longing to lie on tidal sand or be

Mixed with the salty water strange and cold.
And, out of dingy room in London, dart
Forth out toward the wide
Horizon that is always in the heart,
Watch the slow-coming, slow retreating tide.

O, pack your bag and go away with me
Down to some little town beside the sea.

THE HOPELESS ARGUMENT

I SAW two old men sitting by a stove,
Repeating loud illustrious stories
Of blood, and half-forgotten glories.

I said: "You seem discursive. What of love?"
One said: "It is a most distressing thing."
The other, without teeth, began to sing.

So to those old men sitting by that fire,
Trying to warm their hopeless shaking fists,
Dibbing and cuffing their unhappy wrists,

I said: "Oh, what then of our great desire?"
One cried: "Desire is certainly no matter."
The other's crumbling jaws began to chatter.

Then I stared down on them with bitter eyes,
For I was young, and so they wished me dead;
This being wrong, contemptuously I said:

148

"You are too old for love, but not for lies."
Shivering, one put on his tattered hat;
The other leant across the fire and spat.

SEED-TIME OUTSIDE EDEN

He

NOW, while I scatter seed, you wait,
And scare the birds, beside that gate.
The task is hard I have to do:
It is an easy one for you
There in the shade to sit and sing,
And keep those large flocks on the wing.

She

Why are you always busy now?
The grain, the harvest, or the plough
Take all the spirit from your kiss.
Leave sowing. Your glad love I miss.
Or if my singing has become
A cry to scare the birds, I'm dumb.
Do as you must. I will not stay
To help you. I will sleep to-day.

He

Ah! you don't mind about the grain:
So my whole work may be in vain.
I know my duty, and will do
All that I can, in spite of you.

The seed is burning in my hand,
And lusting for the fertile land.

She

Come and lie underneath this tree,
And plant your human seed in me.
Make in my fertile body first
The crop for which my senses thirst.

He

I come to you because you call,
And to your passionate word I fall.
But the whole time we satiate
Our flesh, I fear the after-hate.

She

Fear nothing. Pass your hands along
My body. Hold me. You are strong.
Cast that unfeeling bag of seed
Away. Now satisfy our need.
I hate the interfering wheat.
Oh, there will be enough to eat.

AT MIDNIGHT

I WANT to leave the ugly town,
Where people talk all night, and all day.
To-morrow I'll be lying down
Snug in the hay.

I'll take my large and crooked stick,
Close all my books and quickly go;
Then I'll be sleeping in a rick,
And nobody shall know.

My friends will talk of me a while,
Tell most sarcastic tales and *Hem!*
I shall not even need to smile:
I shall not think at all of them.

I shall be listening to a wind
Far more melodious than their chatter;
I shall have my industrious mind
Absorbed in more important matter.

   .   .   .   .   .

It is a most delightful dream
To leave them and their ugly faces,
And wander by a shining stream
To happy and more happy places.

But I can hear the trams that gride
Along their shiny rails outside.

And now I must be comforted
With laying my unhappy head
Quietly on its London bed.

OFFICERS' MESS (1916)

I

I SEARCH the room with all my mind,
Peering among those eyes;

For I am feverish to find
A brain with which my brain may talk,
Not that I think myself too wise,
But that I'm lonely, and I walk
Round the large place and wonder—No:
There's nobody, I fear,
Lonely as I, and here.

How they hate me. I'm a fool.
I can't play Bridge; I'm bad at Pool;
I cannot drone a comic song;
I can't talk Shop; I can't use Slang;
My jokes are bad, my stories long:
My voice will falter, break or hang,
Not blurt the sour sarcastic word,
And so my swearing sounds absurd.

II

But came the talk: I found
Three or four others for an argument.
I forced their pace. They shifted their dull ground,
And went
Sprawling about the passages of Thought.
We tugged each other's words until they tore.
They asked me my philosophy: I brought
Bits of it forth and laid them on the floor.
They laughed, and so I kicked the bits about,
Then put them in my pocket one by one,
I, sorry I had brought them out,
They, grateful for the fun.

And when these words had thus been sent
Jerking about, like beetles round a wall,

Then one by one to dismal sleep we went:
There was no happiness at all
In that short hopeless argument
Through yawns and on the way to bed
Among men waiting to be dead.

CHILDREN OF LOVE

THE holy boy
Went from his mother out in the cool of the day
Over the sun-parched fields
And in among the olives shining green and shining grey.

There was no sound,
No smallest voice of any shivering stream.
Poor sinless little boy,
He desired to play, and to sing; he could only sigh and
    dream.

Suddenly came
Running along to him naked, with curly hair,
That rogue of the lovely world,
That other beautiful child whom the virgin Venus bare.

The holy boy
Gazed with those sad blue eyes that all men know.
Impudent Cupid stood
Panting, holding an arrow and pointing his bow.

(Will you not play?
Jesus, run to him, run to him, swift for our joy.

Is he not holy, like you?
Are you afraid of his arrows, O beautiful dreaming boy?)

And now they stand
Watching one another with timid gaze;
Youth has met youth in the wood,
But holiness will not change its melancholy ways.

Cupid at last
Draws his bow and softly lets fly a dart.
Smile for a moment, sad world!—
It has grazed the white skin and drawn blood from the
    sorrowful heart.

Now, for delight,
Cupid tosses his locks and goes wantonly near;
But the child that was born to the cross
Has let fall on his cheek, for the sadness of life, a com-
    passionate tear.

Marvellous dream!
Cupid has offered his arrows for Jesus to try;
He has offered his bow for the game.
But Jesus went weeping away, and left him there wondering
    why.

OVERHEARD ON A SALTMARSH

NYMPH, nymph, what are your beads?
Green glass, goblin. Why do you stare at them?
Give them me.
              No.

Give them me. Give them me.
                    No.
Then I will howl all night in the reeds,
Lie in the mud and howl for them.

Goblin, why do you love them so?

They are better than stars or water,
Better than voices of winds that sing,
Better than any man's fair daughter,
Your green glass beads on a silver ring.

Hush I stole them out of the moon.

Give me your beads, I desire them.
                    No.
I will howl in a deep lagoon
For your green glass beads, I love them so.
Give them me. Give them.
                    No.

THE REBELLIOUS VINE

ONE day, the vine
That clomb on God's own house
Cried, "I will not *grow*,"
And, "I will *not* grow,"
And, "I *will* not grow,"
And, "*I* will not grow."
So God leaned out his head,
And said:

"You need not." Then the vine
Fluttered its leaves, and cried to all the winds:
"Oh, have I not permission from the Lord?
And may I not begin to cease to grow?"
But that wise God had pondered on the vine
Before he made it.
And, all the while it laboured *not* to grow,
It grew; it grew;
And all the time God knew.

GREAT CITY

WHEN I returned at sunset,
The serving-maid was singing softly
Under the dark stairs, and in the house
Twilight had entered like a moonray.
Time was so dead I could not understand
The meaning of midday or of midnight,
But like falling waters, falling, hissing, falling,
Silence seemed an everlasting sound.

I sat in my dark room,
And watched sunset,
And saw starlight.
I heard the tramp of homing men,
And the last call of the last child;
Then a lone bird twittered,
And suddenly, beyond the housetops,

I imagined dew in the country,
In the hay, on the buttercups;

The rising moon,
The scent of early night,
The songs, the echoes,
Dogs barking,
Day closing,
Gradual slumber,
Sweet rest.

When all the lamps were lighted in the town
I passed into the streetways, and I watched,
Wakeful, almost happy,
And half the night I wandered in the street.

LONDON INTERIOR

AUTUMN is in the air,
The children are playing everywhere.

One dare not open this old door too wide;
It is so dark inside.
The hall smells of dust;
A narrow squirt of sunlight enters high,
Cold, yellow.
The floor creaks, and I hear a sigh,
Rise in the gloom and die.

Through the hall, far away,
I just can see
The dingy garden with its wall and tree.
A yellow cat is sitting on the wall

Blinking toward the leaves that fall.
And now I hear a woman call
Some child from play.

Then all is still. Time must go
Ticking slow, glooming slow.

The evening will turn grey.
It is sad in London after two.
All, all the afternoon
What can old men, old women do?

It is sad in London when the gloom
Thickens, like wool,
In the corners of the room;
The sky is shot with steel,
Shot with blue.

The bells ring the slow time;
The chairs creak, the hours climb;
The sunlight lays a streak upon the floor.

HEARTHSTONE

I WANT nothing but your fireside now.
Friend, you are sitting there alone I know,
And the quiet flames are licking up the soot,
Or crackling out of some enormous root:
All the logs on your hearth are four feet long.
Everything in your room is wide and strong
According to the breed of your hard thought.

Now you are leaning forward; you have caught
That great dog by his paw and are holding it,
And he looks sidelong at you, stretching a bit,
Drowsing with open eyes, huge, warm and wide,
The full hearth-length on his slow-breathing side.
Your book has dropped unnoticed: you have read
So long you cannot send your brain to bed.
The low quiet room and all its things are caught
And linger in the meshes of your thought.
(Some people think they know time cannot pause).
Your eyes are closing now though not because
Of sleep. You are searching something with your brain;
You have let the old dog's paw drop down again. . . .
Now suddenly you hum a little catch,
And pick up the book. The wind rattles the latch;
There's a patter of light cool rain and the curtain shakes;
The silly dog growls, moves, and almost wakes.
The kettle near the fire one moment hums.
Then a long peace upon the whole room comes.
So the sweet evening will draw to its bedtime end.
I want nothing now but your fireside, friend.

SUBURB

DULL and hard the low wind creaks
Among the rustling pampas plumes.
Drearily the year consumes
Its fifty-two insipid weeks.

Most of the grey-green meadow land
Was sold in parsimonious lots;
The dingy houses stand

Pressed by some stout contractor's hand
Tightly together in their plots.

Through builded banks the sullen river
Gropes, where its houses crouch and shiver.
Over the bridge the tyrant train
Shrieks, and emerges on the plain.

In all the better gardens you may pass,
(Product of many careful Saturdays),
Large red geraniums and tall pampas grass
Adorn the plots and mark the gravelled ways.

Sometimes in the background may be seen
A private summer-house in white or green.
Here on warm nights the daughter brings
Her vacillating clerk,
To talk of small exciting things
And touch his fingers through the dark.

He, in the uncomfortable breach
Between her trilling laughters,
Promises, in halting speech,
Hopeless immense Hereafters.

She trembles like the pampas plumes.
Her strained lips haggle. He assumes
The serious quest. . . .

Now as the train is whistling past
He takes her in his arms at last.

It's done. She blushes at his side
Across the lawn—a bride, a bride.

The stout contractor will design,
The lazy labourers will prepare,
Another villa on the line;
In the little garden-square
Pampas grass will rustle there.

APPOINTMENT

I SAID seven o'clock:
You are there, O you fool.
The floating air of the summer is cool;
You delight in the drift of your white frock.

And I am secure in the gloom.
Your waiting thoughts are remembering my face—
Which reclines in a secret contented grimace
In my lonely room.

I am thinking so hard of you. How I prefer
To imagine you here, without trouble or stir.
Anger is now beginning to tinge
Your temples below that careful fringe.

You were tolerant always. Your female control
Was designed and expressed
In every gasping sign of soul
You ever confessed.

I followed for long like a dog on the leather.
I knew all the time all the tricks of your plot.
We wandered the ways of the summer together.
I knew what you were—and what you are not.

Now walk in the twilight. I'm here
Contented. Your hour
Is finished. I am without fear
Of your beauty or hopeless power.

Come to me, if you dare! Come! Who
Is knocking? Who's there? Come in.
I'm alone you see. Oh, it's you.
I was reading a book. I was not
Thinking. It's late. I forgot.
Are you ill? You are thin.
I am sorry. What? Well . . .
Sit down. We've heaps to tell
Each other. Let's begin.
I am glad you have come. Let me fold
You close in my arms. You are cold.

MILK FOR THE CAT

WHEN the tea is brought at five o'clock,
And all the neat curtains are drawn with care,
The little black cat with bright green eyes
Is suddenly purring there.

At first she pretends, having nothing to do,
She has come in merely to blink by the grate,
But, though tea may be late or the milk may be sour,
She is never late.

And presently her agate eyes
Take a soft large milky haze,

And her independent casual glance
Becomes a stiff hard gaze.

Then she stamps her claws or lifts her ears
Or twists her tail and begins to stir,
Till suddenly all her lithe body becomes
One breathing trembling purr.

The children eat and wriggle and laugh;
The two old ladies stroke their silk:
But the cat is grown small and thin with desire,
Transformed to a creeping lust for milk.

The white saucer like some full moon descends
At last from the clouds of the table above;
She sighs and dreams and thrills and glows,
Transfigured with love.

She nestles over the shining rim,
Buries her chin in the creamy sea;
Her tail hangs loose; each drowsy paw
Is doubled under each bending knee.

A long dim ecstasy holds her life;
Her world is an infinite shapeless white,
Till her tongue has curled the last holy drop,
Then she sinks back into the night,

Draws and dips her body to heap
Her sleepy nerves in the great arm-chair,
Lies defeated and buried deep
Three or four hours unconscious there.

THE DEPARTURE

GOD, I've stayed, thy hated guest,
  In thy tavern far too long.
I desire a little rest
  From thy sermon and thy song.
Frown no more to me of sin:
  Evil for the evil heart. ˙
To the tavern of my kin
  I am ready to depart.

We have found a stronger wine,
  (For most bibulous are we.)
Every vineyard is not thine
  Over all eternity.
God, thou melancholy host,
  Greybeard without any jest,
Make it never more thy boast
That I linger like a ghost
  In thy tavern as thy guest.

THE POETS ARE WAITING

TO what God
Shall we chant
Our songs of Battle?

The professional poets
Are measuring their thoughts
For felicitous sonnets;

They try them and fit them
Like honest tailors
Cutting materials
For fashion-plate suits.

The unprofessional
Little singers,
Most intellectual,
Merry with gossip,
Heavy with cunning,
Whose tedious brains are draped
In sultry palls of hair,
Reclining as usual
On armchairs and sofas,
Are grinning and gossiping,
Cake at their elbows—
They will not write us verses for the time;
Their storms are brewed in teacups and their wars
Are fought in sneers or little blots of ink.

To what God
Shall we chant
Our songs of Battle?

Hefty barbarians,
Roaring for war,
Are breaking upon us;
Clouds of their cavalry,
Waves of their infantry,
Mountains of guns.
Winged they are coming,
Plated and mailed,
Snorting their jargon.
Oh, to whom shall a song of battle be chanted?

Not to our lord of the hosts on his ancient throne,
Drowsing the ages out in Heaven alone.
The celestial choirs are mute, the angels have fled:
Word is gone forth abroad that our lord is dead.

To what God
Shall we chant
Our songs of battle?

YOUTH IN ARMS

I

HAPPY boy, happy boy,
David the immortal willed,
Youth a thousand thousand times
Slain, but not once killed,
Swaggering again to-day
In the old contemptuous way;

Leaning backward from your thigh
Up against the tinselled bar—
Dust and ashes! is it you?
Laughing, boasting, there you are!
First we hardly recognised you
In your modern avatar.

Soldier, rifle, brown khaki—
Is your blood as happy so?
Where's your sling, or painted shield,
Helmet, pike, or bow?
Well, you're going to the wars—
That is all you need to know.

166

Greybeards plotted. They were sad.
Death was in their wrinkled eyes.
At their tables, with their maps
Plans and calculations, wise
They all seemed; for well they knew
How ungrudgingly Youth dies.

At their green official baize
They debated all the night
Plans for your adventurous days
Which you followed with delight,
Youth in all your wanderings,
David of a thousand slings.

II

SOLDIER

Are you going? To-night we must all hear your laughter;
We shall need to remember it in the quiet days after.
Lift your rough hands, grained like unpolished oak.
Drink, call, lean forward, tell us some happy joke.
Let us know every whim of your brain and innocent soul.
Your speech is let loose; your great loafing words roll
Like hill-waters. But every syllable said
Brings you nearer the time you'll be found lying dead
In a ditch, or rolled stiff on the stones of a plain.
(Thought! Thought go back into your kennel again:
Hound, back!) Drink your glass, happy soldier, to-night.
Death is quick; you will laugh as you march to the fight.
We are wrong. Dreaming ever, we falter and pause:
You go forward unharmed without Why or Because.
Spring does not question. The war is like rain;
You will fall in the field like a flower without pain;
And who shall have noticed one sweet flower that dies?
The rain comes; the leaves open, and other flowers rise.

167

The old clock tolls. Now all our words are said.
We drift apart and wander away to bed.
We dream of War. *Your* closing eyelids keep
Quiet watch upon your heavy dreamless sleep.
You do not wonder if you shall, nor why,
If you must, by whom, for whom, you will die.
You are snoring. (The hound of thought by every breath
Brings you nearer for us to your foreign death.)

Are you going? Good-bye, then, to that last word you
    spoke
We must try to remember you best by some happy joke.

                      III
RETREAT
That is not war—oh it hurts! I am lame.
A thorn is burning me.
We are going back to the place from which we came.
I remember the old song now:

        Soldier, soldier, going to war,
        When will you come back?

Mind that rut. It is very deep.
All these ways are parched and raw.
Where are we going? How we creep!
Are you there? I never saw—

Damn this jingle in my brain.
I'm full of old songs—Have you ever heard this?

        All the roads to victory
        Are flooded as we go.

There's so much blood to paddle through,
That's why we're marching slow.

Yes sir; I'm here. Are you an officer?
I can't see. Are we running away?
How long have we done it? One whole year,
A month, a week, or since yesterday?

Damn the jingle. My brain
Is scragged and banged—

> *Fellows, these are happy times;*
> *Tramp and tramp with open eyes.*
> *Yet, try however much you will,*
> *You cannot see a tree, a hill,*
> *Moon, stars, or even skies.*

I won't be quiet. Sing too, you fool.
I had a dog I used to beat.
Don't try it on me. Say that again.
Who said it? *Halt!* Why? Who can halt?
We're marching now. Who fired? Well. Well.
I'll lie down too. I'm tired enough.

IV

CARRION

It is plain now what you are. Your head has dropped
Into a furrow. And the lovely curve
Of your strong leg has wasted and is propped
Against a ridge of the ploughed land's watery swerve.

You are swayed on waves of the silent ground;
You clutch and claim with passionate grasp of your fingers

The dip of earth in which your body lingers;
If you are not found,
In a little while your limbs will fall apart;
The birds will take some, but the earth will take most
    your heart.

You are fuel for a coming spring if they leave you here;
The crop that will rise from your bones is healthy bread.
You died—we know you—without a word of fear,
And as they loved you living I love you dead.

No girl would kiss you. But then
No girls would ever kiss the earth
In the manner they hug the lips of men:
You are not known to them in this, your second birth.

No coffin-cover now will cram
Your body in a shell of lead;
Earth will not fall on you from the spade with a slam,
But will fold and enclose you slowly, you living dead.

Hush, I hear the guns. Are you still asleep?
Surely I saw you a little heave to reply.
I can hardly think you will not turn over and creep
Along the furrows trenchward as if to die.

THE STRANGE COMPANION
(*A Fragment*)

THAT strange companion came on shuffling feet,
Passed me, then turned, and touched my arm.

He said (and he was melancholy,
And both of us looked fretfully,
And slowly we advanced together)
He said: "I bring you your inheritance."

I watched his eyes; they were dim.
I doubted him, watched him, doubted him . . .
But, in a ceremonious way,
He said: "You are too grey:
Come, you must be merry for a day."

And I, because my heart was dumb,
Because the life in me was numb,
Cried: "I will come. I *will* come."

So, without another word,
We two jaunted on the street.
I had heard, often heard,
The shuffling of those feet of his,
The shuffle of his feet.

And he muttered in my ear
Such a wheezy jest
As a man may often hear—
Not the worst, not the best
That a man may hear.

Then he murmured in my face
Something that was true.
He said: "I have known this long, long while,
All there is to know of you."
And the light of the lamp cut a strange smile
On his face, and we muttered along the street,
Good enough friends, on the usual beat.

We lived together long, long.
We were always alone, he and I.
We never smiled with each other;
We were like brother and brother,
Dimly accustomed.
                              Can a man know
Why he must live, or whether he should go?

He brought me that joke or two,
And we roared with laughter, for want of a smile,
As every man in the world might do.

He who lies all night in bed
Is a fool, and midnight will crush his head.

When he threw a glass of wine in my face
One night, I hit him, and we parted;
But in a short space
We came back to each other melancholy hearted,
Told our pain,
Swore we would not part again.

One night we turned a table over
The body of some slain fool to cover,
And all the company clapped their hands;
So we spat in their faces,
And travelled away to other lands.

I wish for every man he find
A strange companion so
Completely to his mind
With whom he everywhere may go.

THE VIRGIN

ARMS that have never held me; lips of him
Who should have been for me; hair most beloved,
I would have smoothed so gently; steadfast eyes,
Half-closed, yet gazing at me through the dusk;
And hands—you sympathetic human hands,
I would have everlastingly adored,
To which I have so often tendered mine
Across the gulf, O far, far, far away
Unwilling hands; and voice of him I have dreamed
So often in the evening by the fire,
Whose step I have heard approaching, at the door
Pausing, but never entering: O tall
And well-beloved imaginary form—
I curse you! Is the silence of the night
Not mine, but you must haunt it? Are my dreams
Not mine, but you must fill them? There were days
I had some little beauty for you—Why
Came you not then? What kept you? Now my lips
Are feverish with longing, and mine eyes,
Wanton with expectation. Where are you?
In what moon-haunted garden? By what stream?
Where whisper you your vows? Among what flowers,
(Which bloom though I am barren)? To what maid
Of cream and rose in muslin?—And her hand
Touches you lightly, while you tremble. She
Had waited also; but you came to her.
I would not be revengeful—yet of late
I dream of every maiden I behold,
She may have won you from me. Oh, believe!
None other can have loved you as I would.
So long, so long have I imagined you;

Yea, from my foolish girlhood, every night
Have held you in my arms. Forgive me, love!
You seemed so nearly mine; and every morning
I cried "To-day!" And often in my prayers
When I would try to think of Jesus Christ,
It only seemed as if I thought of you.
Oh, surely I deserved some better fate
Than this black barren destitution. I
Am made of flesh, and I have tingling nerves:
My blood is always hot, and I desire
The touch of gentle hands upon my face
To cool it, as the moonlight cools the earth.
There is no peace. In spring, the turtle doves
Madden me with their crooning, and the trees
Whisper all day together. Everywhere
There is some festival of love. Alas,
Men in all places openly declare
Love is the world, and maidens, with a blush,
Hint beautiful devotion. Know they not
I am a woman—I could too have served?
Sometimes (young matrons look upon me so),
I laugh aloud in everybody's face
Instead of weeping, for I have to choose
Quickly. That sudden laugh without a cause
Has grown into a habitude of late:
Thus people stare at me, and shake their heads,
And sign to one another with their eyes.
Then afterwards I always have to go
Alone to drench my pillow with my tears. . . .
You, you, who have not loved me, who have found
Some other consolation in the world,
Who are my cause and complement of woe,
Say, what can be achieved through such as I?
I cannot change the pattern of my soul.

It surely is not evil to desire:
Mothers desire their children, and the priest
Desires his God; the earth desires the sun;
And I lean out in agony for you;
So very long I had expected you:
I was not wanton till you did not come.
Whoever you may be, hear me at last!
Faintly, I do implore you for your hands:
I grope to find them. Stay! I have become
So humble now, that meekly I will follow
Whatever way you lead me through the world.
I have no habitation of my own.
Unsacred is my room, mine images
Unconsecrated, and my lonely bed
Haunted with memories of the wakeful night
All void of love, and of the barren dawn.
It is so weary to begin the days,
To stir, wake, wonder, rise, and breathe again:
O how much longer must I tolerate
The flowerless repetition of the hours,
And little occupations without cause?
Love! Love! I want to lay my body out,
To be all covered over, to receive;
I want to hold, and fasten, and be held:
I hunger; I am starved. . . . And I have thought
Sometimes men gazed upon me half in fear,
As though they guessed my hunger. Gracious God!
I am not vile: I only would obey
Thy law, as thine own stars obey—they rush
Love-swift together, and a million suns
Proceed from that embrace. The stars! Indeed
The filthy worm that feeds upon the corpse
Obeys thee also—loves, and is beloved;
Yet I must clasp my cold hands desperately,

Feed on my strained flesh, and my captive soul
Must beat against the black bars. I was born
Through love; I was created by the law
That makes the low worm equal with the stars:
My father held my mother in his arms,
And while she trembled with delight of him,
I was conceived, and holy was the hour—
But I shall die for want of being loved.
Truly it is not just. With my despair
I am a creature so lascivious now,
That no one anywhere is safe. Mine eyes
Wander and rest, and wander and devour.
I meditate on subtle-hearted plans,
And small deceits, and rasping jealousies.
My voice is sour or bitter, and I blush
Suddenly without reason, or I hang
For reassurance on some trivial words
Spoken in jest, or suddenly I feel
Covered with guilty shame, and swift must go
To drench my lonely pillow with my tears.
Or I seek out the mirror, with mine eyes
To gaze in mine own eyes, and smooth my hair,
Or sometimes to adorn it with a rose,
Imagining I may be beautiful.
Indeed, indeed, my hair is very black,
My skin most white—most pallid. . . . O you powers
That guard the destiny of woman, you
Have wronged me somehow: surely you have erred.
What consolation have you left for me ?
Indeed I had been worthy of some love:
I cannot keep my thoughts away from that,
That always—for my life is on the leash:
I have not ever yet begun to live.
But after benediction of warm arms,

After delight of consecrative hands,
After firm, hot and sympathetic lips
Pressed hard upon me—afterward my flesh
Had leapt to vigour; my disjointed thoughts
Had followed one another in stern train
Of consequence. My life would have begun:
I should have been beloved. . . . Alas! Oh God!
God! Where has passion led me? To what shame!
I have become a harlot in my thoughts.
I am no fit companion for myself.
I must begin again, must wash my soul,
Accept my fate in silence, and be pure.
There *is* some consolation. Have I not
Neglected my devotion? I must pray.
Will He not help me if I pray to Him?
Are there not many virgins in the world
Who yield their spirits to Him, and so remain
Silent, reflective, beautiful? But I
Rage like a wanton. Though the days be long,
And God seem always absent, though the nights
Be longer; nevertheless I will be pure. . . .
Yet know I many mothers without taint;
Silent, reflective, beautiful are they,
Being beloved—and surely they are pure.
God! God! You are not just, for you yourself
Were known unto a virgin, and your son
Was born, and you had your delight therein.
You are not just, and your Heaven is too far;
I cannot fix my countenance on you:
I have too much devotion for the earth.
You should descend upon me, for I gasp
To hold and to possess some living form.

Alas! My life is dragging from its prime.
My days are bitter with salt tears. Lo, I
Shall pass into the shadow, and the gloom
Will fold me hard about.   I shall decay
Slowly like withered flowers.   The atmosphere
Will sicken all around me. I shall droop
Towards the tomb, shall stumble, and shall fall.
My body will be covered with rank earth.
My nostrils will be stopped. I shall remain
Alone and unbeloved for evermore.

GO NOW, BELOVED

GO now, beloved! I too desire it thus.
Go swiftly! but you cannot break the chain.
Fate hath the bitter lordship over us:
        Go now—in vain!

When you are in his arms at dead of night,
Safe in the darkness, though you cannot see,
Sudden shall flash upon your inward sight
        The form of me.

My image will be present in the air:
Though you may strive your weariest to be true,
I, where the sunrays on the carpet flare,
        Shall rise for you.

When you and he together in the spring
At sunset by your open doorway stand,

You shall grow faint, too much remembering
            My voice and hand.

When he shall bring you roses, this last hour
Shall snatch their beauty from you like a thief;
For there shall be remembrance in each flower,
            Stem, thorn and leaf.

Slow year by year I shall become more true,
Until I never leave you day nor night;
Shall faithfully take my station between you
            And all delight.

When he shall pass his fingers through your hair,
However gentle you may be and fond,
Your gaze shall not meet his—your eyes will stare
            At me beyond.

Nor will your agony for me be told,
And peacefully put aside when you must die:
Though all remembrance of your youth grow cold—
            Yet will not I.

I will so haunt you to the verge of death,
That when, in bitterness of spirit, he
Shall lean across you, you with your last breath
Shall call for me.

Go now, belovèd—but remember, past
The limits of terrestrial love or hate,
I, at the portal of the unknown vast,
            Shall, silent, wait.

PARADISE

BELOVÈD, I had given you my soul,
(Which is my body): you and I had dwelt
One year in paradise—when God appeared.
He saw us very simple: we would pass
Whole days in contemplation of some thought
Frail as a white narcissus. We desired
The earth, and found the beauty of the earth
In one another. We had paradise,
And would have dwelt eternally therein,
Had God not, in the likeness of a snake,
Crept in between us, had he not become
Jealous as he is wont. Alas! Alas!
Belovèd, evil are the ways of God.
Let us not fear him, nor with suppliant hands
Ask any mercy from him out of heaven.
He gave us not this dreaming love of ours,
Nor paradise, nor any flower therein:
Nor shall he take them from us.   He is God
Sole and elect of all the world outside,
And I had seen him roaming at the dusk
In the semblance of a man, cunning and huge,
Jealously round the gates, before he crept
Between us like a serpent, and declared
He would barter all the gold he holds in heaven
For one frail flower of paradise.   Belovèd,
Let us continue children of the earth
Among the simple flowers—tall lilies, pansies,
And white narcissus; for a little care
They fill the night with perfume: and if God
Breaks in upon us by some strategem,
Let us remain apart with silent eyes,

Not fearing, scarce perceiving, to ourselves
Complete in one another till the end.
The tread of God is murder: if he comes
Pursuing us with vengeance, let us stand
Together, silent still, against some tree,
Whose sacred life we shall be conscious of
Within trunk, boughs and leaves. Thus let us pass,
If need be underneath the foot of God,
Back to the everlasting, out of which
We have, beloved, this little season dwelt
Together with our flowers in paradise.

AT A COUNTRY DANCE IN PROVENCE

COMRADES, when the air is sweet,
It is fair, in stately measure,
With a sound of gliding feet,
It is fair and very meet
To be joined in pleasure.
Listen to the rhythmic beat:
Let us mingle, move and sway
Solemnly as at some rite
Of a festive mystic god,
While the sunlight holds the day.
Comrades, is it not delight
To be governed by the rod
Of the music, and to go
Moving, moving, moving slow?
Very stately are your ways,

Stately—and the southern glow
Of the sun is in your eyes:
Under lids inclining low
All the light of harvest days,
And the gleam of summer skies
Tenderly reflected lies.
May I not be one of you
Even for this little space?
Humbly I am fain to sue
That our arms may interlace.
I am otherwise I know;
Many books have made me sad:
Yet indeed your stately slow
Motion and its rhythmic flow
Drive me, drive me, drive me mad.
Must I now, as always, gaze
Patiently from far away
At the pageant of the days?—
Only let me live to-day!
For your hair is ebon black,
And your eyes celestial blue;
For your measure is so true,
Slowly forward, slowly back—
I would fain be one of you.
Comrades, comrades! but the sound
Of the music with a start
Ceases, and you pass me by.
Slowly from the dancing-ground
To the tavern you depart.
All the earth is silent grown
After so much joy, and I
Suddenly am quite alone
With the beating of my heart.

LAKE LEMAN

IT is the sacred hour: above the far
Low emerald hills that northward fold,
Calmly, upon the blue, the evening star
Floats, wreathed in dusky gold.
The winds have sung all day; but now they lie
Faint, sleeping; and the evening sounds awake.
The slow bell tolls across the water: I
Am haunted by the spirit of the lake.
It seems as though the sounding of the bell
Intoned the low song of the water-soul,
And at some moments I can hardly tell
The long resounding echo from the toll.
The spirit of the water is awake:
O thou mysterious lake,
Thou art enchanted, and thy spell
Holds all who round thy fruitful margin dwell.
Oft have I seen home-going peasants' eyes
Lit with the peace that emanates from thee.
Those who among thy waters plunge, arise
Filled with new wisdom and serenity.
What knowledge, what remembrance can have thus
Set beauty for a token on thy brow?
Lake that I love, whence comest thou to us?—
So strange and wistful in our midst art thou.
Thy veins are in the mountains. I have heard,
Down-stretched beside thee at the silent noon,
With leaning head attentive to thy word,
A secret and delicious mountain-tune,
Proceeding as from many shadowed hours
In ancient forests carpeted with flowers,
And, farther still, where trickling waters haunt

Between the crevices of white crags gaunt.
Ah, what repose at breathless noon to go,
Lean on thy bosom, hold thee with stretched hands,
And listen for the music of the snow!
But most, as now,
When harvest covers thy surrounding lands,
I love thee, with a coronal of sheaves
Crowned regent of the day;
And on the air thy placid breathing leaves
A scent of corn and hay.
For thou hast gathered (as a mother will
The sayings of her children in her heart),
The harvest-thoughts of reapers on the hill,
When the cool rose and honeysuckle fill
The air, and fruit is laden on the cart.
Thou breathest the delight
Of summer evening at the deep-roofed farm,
And meditation of the summer night,
When the enravished earth is lying warm
From recent kisses of the conquering sun.
Dwell as a spirit in me, O thou one
Sweet natural presence. In the years to be
When all the mortal loves perchance are done,
Them I will bid farewell, but, oh, not thee.
I love thee. When the youthful visions fade,
Fade thou not also in the hopeless past.
Be constant and delightful, as a maid
Sought over all the world, and found at last.

IMPRESSIONS

I

AT sunrise, on the lonely way,
He looms against the fiery sky,

As, to the labour of the day,
I watch him eagerly go by.

His scythe, upon his shoulder borne,
Points weirdly to the gathering light:
He is a symbol of the Morn
Emerging from unconscious night.

And unto him the sacred field
Gives bread to sanctify the feast;
He is the honour of the yield;
We are the suppliants, he the priest.

II

He's something in the city. Who shall say
His fortune was not honourably won?
Few people can afford to give away
As he, or help the poor as he has done.

Neat in his habits, temperate in his life:
Oh, who shall dare his character besmirch?
He scarcely ever quarrels with his wife
And every sabbath strictly goes to church.

He helps the village club, and in the town
Attends parochial meetings once a week,
Pays for each purchase ready-money down:
Is anyone against him?—Who will speak?

There is a widow somewhere in the north,
On whom slow ruin gradually fell,
While she, believing that her God was wrath,
Suffered without a word—or she might tell.

And there's a beggar somewhere in the west,
Whose fortune vanished gradually away:
Now he but drags his limbs in horror lest
Starvation feed on them—or he might say.

And there are children stricken with disease,
Too ignorant to curse him, or too weak.
In a true portrait of him all of these
Must figure in the background—they shall speak.

III

I saw him at the Carlton in his wine.
His white broad hand along the table lay.
A waiter passed a savory made of swine
On scraps of pastry, which he waved away,
Then looked about him over his pince-nez.

He carried all the while a genial air
Of infinite patience through that weary meal,
Stroking at moments his well-parted hair,
Or fumbling at his waistcoat, where a seal
Hung from the pocket, like a cotton-reel.

At last his friend beside him, who had read
Two or three times the evening paper through,
And answered to whatever he had said:
"Ah?"—his attention to a column drew,
Murmuring through heavy lips: "Can this be true?"

He took the paper patiently, with like
Patience began to read it and to carve
A shilling strawberry. 'Twas about the strike—
A hundred, in the cause, had sworn to starve.
He put it down, and muttered: "Let them starve!"

IV

Few touches with discriminating art
Correctly set in order, should describe
The stature, the appearance, and the heart
Of him, and every member of his tribe.

His nose is straight, high, narrow, slightly pink;
His hair is brushed and parted without flaw;
His eye has just a trifle of a wink;
His chin—I cannot see enough to draw.

His evening coat curves inward at the waist;
His trousers are immaculately pressed;
His tie is quite correct; in perfect taste
Both shape and buttons of his evening vest.

His boots are patent leather—very smart.
He's highly born and excellently fed.
There's little, very little in his heart,
And absolutely nothing in his head.

V

She comes upon a cool September morn:
I know her by her yellow braided hair,
And by the burden she is wont to bear,
In her strong arms, of precious fruit and corn.

She softly steps across the mellow fields,
Clothed in sweet mist, and followed by a sound
Like dropping of ripe fruit upon the ground:
The world is heavy with its dreams, and yields.

> Oh, where is spring, when all the torrents flow;
> And where is summer, and the sacred glow
> Of heat, long, long ago?—Ah, long ago!

Tune the sad lute, and sing a mournful lay.
Lo, in the forest all the trees have wept
Upon the sodden ground where she has stept—
Slow Autumn on her melancholy way.

VI

So wayward is the wind to-night,
'Twill send the planets tumbling down;
And all the waving trees are dight
In gauzes wafted from the moon.

Faint streaky wisps of roaming cloud
Are swiftly from the mountains swirled;
The wind is like a floating shroud
Wound light about the shivering world.

I think I see a little star
Entangled in a knotty tree,
As trembling fishes captured are
In nets from the eternal sea.

There seems a bevy in the air
Of spirits from the sparkling skies:
There seems a maiden with her hair
All tumbled in my blinded eyes.

Oh, how they whisper, how conspire,
And shrill to one another call!
I fear that, if they cannot tire,
The moon, her shining self, will fall.

Blow! Scatter even if you will
Like spray the stars about mine eyes!
Wind, overturn the goblet, spill
On me the everlasting skies!

JUDAS

JUDAS who sold his lord:—alone he walks
Dream-haunted through the grey, where not a star
Glimmers, nor any dawn breeze whispers hope.
A wilderness surrounds him league on league
Forlorn with desolation to its bounds.
Full in the dreary midst a little lake
Lies stagnant, and above him dusky clouds
Pursue in muffled majesty of woe
A dreary course from east to dreary west.
    I met him on the threshold of a dream,
And felt amid the gloom his startled eyes,
Still luminous with half-forgotten light,
Weary and large from striving to remember;
And then his face, emerging from a mist,
Took gradual form and colour, till I saw
Dimly a red beard flecked with grey, a mouth
Thin-lipped and babbling inarticulate sounds,
Curved nose, thick eyebrows, feathery hair, which lean
Long fingers had dishevelled, last of all
A stooping form and sudden crafty gaze
Sideward.—He hesitated, then he drew
From underneath his raiment something bright,
And, bending over it, into his beard
Muttered, till when, askance, I touched his sleeve,
He looked half up and murmured through his teeth,
"I count my shekels," then: "one, two, three, four"—
To thirty counted. Each was stained with blood.
Lo! as he ceased, the silence of the plain
Suddenly like a whirlwind gathered up,
And broke in one convulsive human shriek,
Trembling and flashing in white agony,

And died; but, swift as thunder after lightning,
Was followed by a roar from east to west
Of human laughter, mocking peal on peal:
And then athwart the still air eagerly
Big drops fell, few at first and very large,
Then more—but they were hot, and more again—
But they were red;—the hissing air was red;
The clouds rained blood:—Shrieks, laughter, then hot
    blood;
And Judas prostrate fell upon the ground,
His thirty shekels scattered, and his arms
Stretched out before him: motionless he lay.
        At length the storm surceased, and once again
An undisturbed stagnation settled down,
Silent, except where, trickling through a cleft,
Some little splashing rivulet of blood
Gurgled and murmured. Judas moved at last,
Strained out a bony-knuckled hand, felt for
And found—his eyes kept hidden—first one piece
Of silver, then another, then a third,
And strained the other hand, then raised his face,
And then his body—slowly standing up.
Blood trickled from his hair and from his arms.
The woe of all the world was in his eyes,
And on his countenance unuttered grief,
Long centuries of silent agony:
Yet, searching in the dust with eager hands,
He gathered up his pieces one by one,
Began to count them through, made twenty-nine—
Searched—found not—raised his eyes, and suddenly
Met mine. Now like a beast he crouched and sprang;
I felt his frigid fingers at my throat,
His long nails, and his breath upon my cheek,
One moment only: then he fell away

And groaned, his features puckered and distort
With hideous avarice. At last he said:
    "Thou hast my silver shekel—give it back!
I cannot yield it now. Once, long ago,
I offered to the master all my wealth:
No merchant makes an offer twice, nor you
Shall steal my money. You are flesh and blood:
I felt my fingers fasten at your throat;
Therefore no spirit are you, like the rest
Who wander on the margin of my land.
You come from trafficking about the world,
From buying and from selling in the mart;
And you have all the earthly ways about you
Of counterfeiting scorn, and lifting up
Your right hand with a movement of disdain,
Shaking your head and turning on your way,
While in your left, secure behind your back,
You hold my shekel.—So, you will not speak!"
    Now suddenly with long arms curved, with hands
Strained, and with breath quick-taken, he advanced
In fury; then his shekel in the dust
Lying half-covered saw. At once he stooped
And swiftly in his two palms gathered it,
And, peering at it, laughed and turned it over,
Till he remembered me; then, screwing up
His crafty eyes, he held it firmly back
Upon his bosom, peeped at it again
Through half-closed hands, and finally drew forth
His other coins: "One, two, three, four, five"—
To thirty counted carefully, his face
Unruffled, as when some dishonest trader
Might calculate his profit: then began
Replacing them, and would have turned, but lo!
Again the silent void was filled with shrieks,

Followed by laughter, last of all with rain
Of hot blood falling. Nor could I awake,
But shrouded in the vision terrible,
Must stand and wonder. Piteously he moaned,
Stretched out his hands imploring my compassion,
And thus began to speak: "Alas! Have you
Not heard my story told in many ways?—
Here is the truth:—At Kerioth I lived;
My father was a merchant. I was sent
Upon his business each Passover feast
North to Jerusalem; himself would go
At the feast of Tabernacles: twice a year
We trafficked in the town. A fashion then
It was among the youth of Kerioth
To delve through olden prophesies, and dream
Of their fulfilment, speculating much
Vainly. I was a leader in my way,
For I could argue always with the laugh
Well on my side: reserving what I called
The hungers of my soul within myself,
Still I could always meet on their own ground
And beat in argument the other youths
Of Kerioth; and I was growing weary
Of forced discussions, certain to diffuse
No clearer light on what I called 'The Truth.'
And well I recollect how in that spring
When first I saw—the master, I had drifted
Into a rash extravagance of thought,
Sworn many times that I would kill myself
Unless I found conclusive answers to
Wild questions that I flung at heaven.—I
Was ruined by such folly in the end."
—He ceased a moment, then with savage eyes:—
"The poison taints my senses even now,

For still when memory gathers in my brain,
I realize that unexpected throb
For sudden beauty. In Jerusalem
I always went to pay the tribute coin
Myself in Herod's temple. From afar
It seemed to float like some entrancèd cloud,
White in the silent blue; and coming near,
One held one's breath a moment in surprise,
And shivered for its beauty. But the courts
At feast time were polluted by the stench
Of cattle driven in from dusty roads,
Foam-flanked upon the burning April day.
Their drovers bargained with the pilgrims, and
Deep in the shadows of the columns sat
Traders and money-changers, greedy-eyed.
All this disgusted me, because I yearned
For that expected kingdom of the Jews:
The long-foreshadowed coming of Messiah,
When joy should be established on the earth—
And this was but a roaring of the beasts.
    Yet in a moment all was changed. 'Twas thus:
While sauntering with nostrils lifted high,
And gazing on the floating roof of gold,
I struck against a pilgrim, who had stooped
For something, and, disdainful when I saw
His occupation, brushing by, passed on.
For he was gathering some stems of rush
Torn from a trampled mat, by accident,
And cast, all vile, into a heap aside.
I noticed as I passed a little band,
Who watched him most intent. One might expect
Strange things in such a crowd—but never this:—
The drovers swearing, traders, raucous-voiced,
Wrangling and teasing, money-changers shrill

With smirking comment, and the rabble coarse,
Complaining—all their mingled voices ceased
A swift astonished moment, then broke out
In one continuous upward sound.—A man
(Not human though he seemed, but more like fire)
Was thrashing all about him right and left
With gathered rushes, overturning here,
Down-treading, scattering confusion there;
Clearing the place alone: a liquid power,
Or breath of God, might be. Then far away
He motionless against a column stood
With parted lips, panting a little, firm,
And speaking not a word; while, cowardly most,
The drovers, traders, money-changers, all
Had fled before him. Soon a few advanced
And challenged him on what authority
He acted thus, while I—I nothing heard,
But trembling on the pavement kissed his feet.
This was the master. What he might have done!"

  He paused again: the sweat was on his brow,
And his imagination was on fire.
Unconscious of the present or of me,
He thus continued:
      "I shall not forget
How in that ecstasy I cast away
Riches, respectability, rank—Life,
All, all I might have had to follow him,
Who should have been a Monarch of the Jews,
Founding the perfect Kingdom on the earth.
God! God! I strove to help Him. Oh! I tried
Up to the last. Oh, what I sacrificed!
  After the feast we straightway journeyed forth,
He and his little band. I left behind
Silently, gladly all my circumstance,

My servants and my custom and my wares;
I never saw my parents once again.
Oh, wonderful the glamour of his eyes!
And lovely seemed the service of the king.
Oh, wonderful the beauty of his face!
He promised the fulfilment of desire;
And everything he uttered was himself:
Oh, wonderful the glamour of his words!
     So we passed northward, dreaming a land
All summer-scented, reaching in the end
The master's country, lovely Galilee.
We prophesied the kingdom. While he preached
We stood about him listening, waiting. When
He hungered we would find him food, and while
He slept we guarded him—the future king.
And once he left us, biding many days
In rugged places fasting and alone.
Then first, far from his gaze and from his speech,
I ruminated much how I could help
His cause, and what achieve—for till that time
I had but followed wondering in the wake
Inactive. There was work, I told myself,
For me. I questioned often. Then a plan
Flashed in upon me. What important step
—I asked myself—could be achieved without
Money—the final key to all success?
And splendid schemes, how he the godly part
And I the necessary worldly share
Of regal duties might perform, took shape.
At once I acted, begged some scanty coin,
And cautiously began to trade. With ease
I doubled it, and trebled it right soon,
(But all in secret, so the little band
Observed me not) and when the master came,

Fresh from God's presence in the wilderness,
Had earned a little treasury of gold
Towards the future kingdom. That was wise.
I wished to tell the master of my plans,
But, somehow, when I saw him, held my peace.
He was so strange unworldly-wise, and all
His dreams were blown from heaven, far-off heaven:
And when he came I ceased from trade a while,
Following in his footsteps silently
From village unto village without gain.
Where he would pass 'twas like a miracle:
So many followed, wondering at his eyes
—Also at what he said; and corpse-like men,
Long ages sick and huddled up with pain,
Would tremble when he spoke and almost spring
To meet his words; and sometimes—for he knew
Some gentle soothing motion—he would chafe
Long while their crippled limbs, till they would stand:
But many crying out: 'A miracle!'
He always left them, passing swift away.
That was the harm. Oh, what he might have done—
Had he but grasped his opportunities;
Not held away from popular applause,
Nor wandered dreaming stealthily about,
But always lived and acted like a king!
—Yet when the fire would flash, to see him then!
He loved that sea of Galilee too well:
Bethsaida, Magdala, Capernaum,
Nazareth too at first; for it was there
He entered in the synagogue to preach,
And knowing him a village carpenter,
They cast him forth (incredulous and rude),
And sought to throw him headlong from the cliff.
But he revealed the beauty of his strength,

Scattering shame among them. 'Twas his way
All patiently to suffer, but sometimes
At last all suddenly to crush. I see
Him now upon the summit of the cliff,
Towering above them like a giant (they thought
He was all meekness), passing through their midst
Quite easily, and leaving them aghast,
Scattered and hesitating, with a few
Cursing him loud. To Nazareth again
He never went. Whole dim unconscious days
He wasted on the shores of Galilee.
But I could not be idle, and what time
He dreamed I carried on a gentle trade:
Working to help his cause. He often thus
Became through long retirements half forgotten
Of those who sought the kingdom. Noise and force
Alone convince the people of the world;
And he who not continually is heard
Is speedily forgotten. This I sought
To tell him once; but Simon, in whose house
He lodged, and called him Peter, came between.
I loathed this Peter with his coarse black hair,
His large blue eyes and grizzly beard: a man
Loud-voiced and powerful without subtlety,
Who could not lie—a stickler for the truth:
Therefore I could not trust him. He it was
Who mockingly proposed one sabbath day
That I, by trade a merchant, should become
Treasurer for the band of brothers. They,
Taking his words in earnest, made him wroth:
And ever after that he hated me.
But I henceforth held openly the funds,
(To aid the master). Who could organize
So well as I amid those simple men?—

197

None had the brains or worldly understanding:
And though I knew the radiance of their light,
The bold transcendent beauty of their dreams,
Their fear of God, yet no important step
Could they have made without me. At the last
They tried and failed, and all that enterprise
Ended in nothing—worse: a shameful death
'Twixt robbers on a tree, and a scattered few
Despised and roaming helpless through the world.
Was ever such an opportunity
For worldly wealth and wisdom to achieve
Some purpose? Very cunning must I act
With these my shekels, when the day is ripe
For such another enterprise."
                                        His face
Clouded despite such utterance. Despair
Belied him, gathering about his lips
In lines and furrows, though unflinchingly
He thus spoke on:
                            "Through me the master's name
Was noised abroad, till one Passover time
(My third as his disciple) he prevailed
So much upon the people that they sought
To crown him king, but he—what think you?—he
Was wroth, and crept away and hid himself.
So in Capernaum, many, when he came,
Left and denied him. I, remaining true,
Strove with him, while his favourite Peter stood
Silent with staring eyes till I had done,
Then turned his back upon me. In the end
I was suspected—yes: the slur of doubt,
Because I magnified the master's cause,
Fell on me. As I looked upon those men
I saw them far away for the first time,

And wondered, were they worthy of my pains?
And doubted, should I cast my life away?
And dreamed of happy Kerioth in the south.
Yet doubts were soon dispelled, and once again
My heart became all rosily suffused
With new device and strategy for him.
I sought his brethren, eagerly implored
Their aid on his behalf: his kith and kin
Desiring much, exhorting much, I thought
Might urge him onward to his goal. They came
Beseeching him with tokens and tears
To journey to Jerusalem with them
Next feast of Tabernacles: they desired
To see him high exalted. He refused,
And waited till the uproar of the time
Was nearly over: then, so to escape
All observation, journeyed there by night,
Hiding by day, and tardily arrived.
Thus many of his party there, ashamed,
Cried out: 'Who are thou?—Hast thou come to rule?'
To which he, vague, as ever was his wont,
Spoke of some perfect kingdom of the clouds,
Out of the present in the far-away,
And argued with them, prophesying much
But doing little. One decisive act
Had won his crown. And still I waited on
Hoping against all hope, my little store
Increasing daily through judicious trade;
And still throughout Jerusalem I noised
His fame, though men would taunt me, speaking thus:
'What people has your master come to rule?
Where is his kingdom?—Not among the Jews!
Is he the party of the Gaulonite?
What hath he said of policies and powers?'

Thus many doubted him, and even sought
To stone him: but he swiftly passed away
Out beyond Jordan—dreaming, dreaming still.
Nevertheless the wonder of his eyes
Was unforgotten, and about his words
There lingered some mysterious delight,
Remembered most when he was far away:
So many sought and many yearned for him,
Saying that soon in purple he would come
To claim his crown.   In Bethany there dwelt
Two women and their brother, whom he loved,
Named Lazarus, concerning whom came news
That he was sick to death. Some impulse burned
Throughout the master's being when he heard,
And, pondering first a little, he passed back
To Bethany with us; and there we learnt
This Lazarus was dead, but, going on
Into his dwelling, found him breathing still.
Then, bending over him with loving touch
And strong inspiring words, as he was wont,
The master filled him with such strength of life
That he arose. Meanwhile I hurried forth
Full of this wonder: in the people's ears
I poured a tale of how their future king
Had brought the dead to life—What could it harm?
He almost might have brought the dead to life,
And that he should was what they most required:
It was the perfect test. Mad with delight,
They, rushing, clamoured round him: all of us,
Even the sisters of the dying man,
Came to believe right soon he had achieved
This very wonder. Lazarus himself
Appeared before the people. Once again

The master fled. In Ephraim for a while
He sojourned; but instinctively I knew
—Or thought I knew—the kingdom was at hand.
His fame passed through Jerusalem. I went
Thither at once to organize affairs,
Taking new courage. Many Pharisees
Spoke eagerly of him, entrusting me
With gold on his behalf. I took it all,
And asked for more, narrating in his cause
The miracle of Lazarus. Meanwhile
A secret council of the Sanhedrin
Was called together—haughty, subtle men:
This, the next day, in confidence I learned,
And learned there was a price upon his head."
　　　Here Judas paused a moment, looking down
And fumbling with the shekels in his hand:
Then thus continued:
　　　　　　　"Very soon I heard
The Master was returning for the feast
Of Passover to Bethany again.
Thither I went to warn him, and to urge
Immediate action. 'Twas with Lazarus
At supper that I found him. As I crept
Into the chamber, tremulous with love,
(So long I had not seen him) at his feet
Mary reclined—the sister—in her hands
Holding a precious alabaster cruse
Of Indian spikenard: I had seen the thing
Before, and knew its value. Slowly now
She poured it out upon the master's feet,
Anointing him, and broke the precious cruse,
And fawned upon him with her hands and hair—
A wanton thriftless woman. Only I
Could understand the spirit of the deed.

While those about him whispered (ignorant!)
And smiled as praising her devotion, I
Cried out: 'For shame! This perfume being sold
Had fetched three hundred pennies for the poor.'
The master gazed a moment. Not a word
Of greeting did he utter. Then they all
Turned on me cold suspicious eyes, while he
Gravely rebuked me for my honest thrift.
I who had starved and stinted for his weal,
I who alone could help him with my gold,
Stood humbled outwardly—but mad within.
So, had I laboured all for such rebuke?
Oh fool! fool! fool! For I was faithful still.
     I soon departed. Now I had resolved
To force him into action, to announce
The kingdom everywhere, say he had power
And gold behind his cause, and that in Rome
Men praised him it was rumoured, that he was
Secretly known of thousands, and to tell
Of plans to shake the universe, to pay
Others to spread report and to proclaim
His miracles: and when the time was ripe
I had resolved to seize him and enthrone him
In majesty and purple. I believed
No human power might ever harm the king
If once he were exalted to the throne
—The saviour long expected, long desired.
Though many spoke of dangers and of dreads;
Of crucifixion, if the Sanhedrin
Could compass his betrayal—what feared I
Trusting Messiah had come! On the next day,
Joyful, along the road to Bethany
I went to meet him coming. In my train
Were Galilean pilgrims, who were prompt

To follow me with anxious zeal. Hard by
The Mount of Olives we perceived him stand
Speaking, erect, his auburn hair blown back
By soft fresh breezes. One could nigh believe
His visage in some radiance enshrined,
And all the fire of God seemed in his eyes.
From those about me went the joyous shout
'Hosanna: hail the Monarch of the Jews!'
And from his little band upon the hill
An answer rose across the morning air.
In triumph to Jerusalem he rode
Upon a colt, I walking at his side,
While hundreds thronged about him. Ardent zeal
Consumed me, and I whispered in his ear
My burning secrets, and my dear resolves:
All, all I would accomplish in his name.
Then I invoked him in the cause of Truth
To rise and take his sceptre and his crown
And set up his pure kingdom on the earth.
Everything I disclosed. He heard me through,
Then gazed, but spoke not—When shall I forget
The look of quiet wonder in his eyes
Or their disdain that froze along my blood!
Then all he said was this: 'The time is come.'
As, sighing, he rode onward. I dropped back,
Like a spent swimmer whom a silent wave
Sweeps over, stifles suddenly, and drowns.
A weariness encompassed me: I went
Pondering long and drearily. Then came
A sudden re-awakening and a light,
With resolution not to cast away
My substance for a shadow. Since he turned
In everything to Peter or to John,
Ignoring me who held the common weal,

They should decide the tenor of his life!
Then, since he always magnified the poor,
I would not sacrifice the gold for him,
Nor strive for him to set a kingdom up;
Not suffer for a king who would not rule.
Was he the Christ—the prophesied Messiah?
He called himself the son of God: yet what
Had he accomplished in the name of God
For us down-trodden Jews? It was foretold
A saviour should accomplish our release,
And I had heard him say Jerusalem
Should be destroyed: this was his kingly way!
I was a Jew, and should I suffer this?
Where was God's Kingdom that he told about
If not a perfect kingdom of the Jews?
Surely he was a dreamer and his band
Blind dreamers following. He had led me far
From duty, from reality. As I,
A youth in Kerioth, had oft become
—Gazing upon the sunset—overpowered
By flame, and, while the moments slip away,
Had, all oblivious, lost my better hold
On Life: so now, three uneventful years,
Held by the fiery beauty of his eyes,
I had forgotten all and followed him.
Yet I would turn to mother world again,
Turn to the human, tangible and real:
Desiring all their worth and excellence.
He would not use the money: it was well—
He should not! I had gotten it, and I
Would keep it as a fraction of that wealth
Which once I sacrificed.—But, looking back
Now even, with my wisdom of the world,
I surely know (so potent was his hold)

Had he but spoken one inspiring word,
He could have had me pouring bitter tears
Of desolate repentance on his feet.
Not so:—he went his way and I went mine,
His to the temple only still to preach
And argue with the Pharisees, and mine
To compass my enfranchisement. The funds
Had risen high. There was a plot of land
North of Jerusalem, a barren tract,
Neglected, waiting for the careful brain,
And ready hand of speculative thrift,
Which often, as I passed it, I had planned
To purchase. Now exactly for a price
Which made the total of the common purse
I bought it—bought my freedom, so it seemed,
Intending to rebuild by careful steps
My shattered fortunes. Sentiment again
Blinded my better vision: I had hoped,
Clearing my senses of the common purse,
To clear them of the master. This performed,
(So rapid are the subtleties of thought)
A change began,—an agony, like shrieks,
Heard distantly yet ringing through my head
Of thousand fiends, and what ideas might burn
One moment in some cranny of my brain,
Ere I could hold them, whirled, and flew away.
Men said I had a devil, for I tore
My garments, wrung my fingers through my hair;
And nowhere could I lay my weary head.
One morning at a corner of the street
Came Simon Peter: I was looking down,
And almost ere I saw him he had passed.
But each turned back as realizing each
A moment late. I met his sea-blue eye:

Immediately he plucked me by the sleeve
Reluctant, saying: 'Truly, brother, thou
Art absent from us long. We need the purse,'
And smiled as in derision, adding: 'Come
To Joseph's house, the counsellor, at even:
For there my master wills we hold the feast.'
Then suddenly a passion caught my breath,
And: 'Not *thy* master,' I replied, 'but *mine*.'
He, laughing yet a little, passed away.
Then how the minutes dragged. A fool I was —
I went of course. The master raised his eyes,
As if he saw his destiny from far
Approaching, and he murmured: 'Thou art come';
But later added, drawing me aside:
'Judas, I do not judge thee. What thou art,
That art thou.' I believe he had divined
The innermost intention of my heart
Ere I had shaped it. Sentimental still,
'Master!'—I cried; but Peter interposed.
And then we supped, and once again he sat
'Twixt John and Peter. Presently his face
Clouded a little, and I heard him say
That someone should betray him. All uprose,
And Peter sanctimoniously outspread
His hands, saying: 'Not I!' Then Jesus turned
To me, amid that company of rude
Uncultured Galileans. As they gazed
Perplexed and foolish on me, all the blood
Ran laughing through my veins. Mysteriously
He handed me a little piece of bread,
Soaked in his wine. Ah, there was freedom in it!
I stared them in the eyes. I was accused,
Judged and condemned: I knew it—and I fled,
Out of the chamber, out into the street,

With Freedom! Freedom! ringing in my ears.
He forced it on me—Why? I could not tell:
I did not care, and still I do not care.
'Twas like the clapping of a prison door
Behind me. Now to feel and kiss the world!
To be sincere: to love myself again!
Now for the trade and traffic of the mart!
Now for the large magnificence of life:
The purple and the splendour and the lust
Of being—Now to be myself again!
And as I went a new refreshing wind
Rushed past me; and joy glittered in all eyes
That peered across the darkness into mine.
When some one stopped me, ardently enquired
Where was the master, I said 'Crucified,'
Nor paused to see the altered countenance:
But onward to the temple! Caiaphas
Had called the Council. Eagerly they snatched
The eager words that darted from my lips,
And thrust upon me (though I craved it not)
Immediate surety :—thirty shekels now;
Three hundred shekels more when he was dead.
Alas! I never held them to their word,
For I was weak. Thus was the bargain made;
The cleverest impostor of the world
Was sold for these, these thirty shekels here.
Go, boast that you have seen them!"
                    Though his speech
Was bold, yet under drooping lids his eyes
Quivered, suspecting I believed him not;
And, seeking to diminish, he increased
My disbelief by adding:
                    "Since that time
I have remembered much, and understood

Much that was dark before or very dim.
I comprehend the dreamer now who hoped
To found the well-constructed world anew,
Yet could not, with his peasants, even raise
Some unavailing kingdom for the Jews.
I know that he eternally was wrong,
I, right: and it is proved by the event.
For now, 'mid those who traffick in the world
How many dream like him? Is not the race
True to the human standard? When in this
Sequestered haunt I hear afar the loud
Shrill wail of splendid suffering, the deep
Strong laughter of ambition; when I feel
The blood of human labour nobly shed,
And all the struggle of it: the robust
Inherent vigour of aspiring man—
Oh, then I know, I know that he was wrong.
      You have not heard the story of my shame,
How my belovèd shekels stung my hand.
'Twas thus: When I had yielded up the man
Who was my master—not to ruminate
Lying abed, or dream, I wandered out
By moonlight on my land, endeavouring
To formulate some speculative scheme
For utmost profit. In the light of dawn
A messenger came running with the news
He was condemned. Then I returned at once
Towards the temple driven by a weak
Distraught idea to have my newer life
Conformably, respectably begun:
I feared some evil luck from this reward,
And, seeking Caiaphas, I cast it down
Upon the pavement, crying, (to my shame),
'The man is innocent of any harm:

I swear it—Let him go!' At first he smiled,
Then, seeing that his fellow-councillors
All frowned, he thundered: 'What is that to us?
See you to it if he is innocent!'
      And bade me take my pieces. So the mood
Passed over for a little, and I woke
From lethargy to business. But, alas!
No more to think precisely nor transact
With certainty of judgment: for a voice
Kept tingling in a corner of my brain
With questions: 'Is the master?' and then,
'Who sold the master?' Singleness of thought
Was gone.—Oh, unavailing human mind
That wanders through perplexity of life
And cannot leave its burden by the way!—
And like the murmuring perpetual wash
Of water was that murmur: 'What of him?'
'What of the master?'—What of him! Now even
It murmurs still, although the greater thought
Of something in the future, some amends,
Following on prosperity again,
Controls it.
                  On a night just such as this
(Save that the moon is hidden by the clouds),
Detained by business late upon my land,
A fever took me—'Twas a barren tract,
And almost treeless—much as this—a lake,
Like that one, near the centre. First the dark
Troubled my vision. Then the glaring moon
Arose and pierced my brain. I never saw
Such light. I wandered aimless. Everything
On earth became revealed: as from afar,
I gazed upon the image of myself;
And hopeless radiance stared me out of thought.

Then soon a cursèd howling wind arose,
And shrieked about the crannies of my soul;
And everything felt dry except the light,
The liquid light of that perpetual moon.
And then that pest of shekels in my hand
Began: I counted, counted them again,
And asked anew their meaning and their end,
And wanted lovely Galilee again,
And questioned why I wanted it, until
The master came to haunt me, and he walked
With Peter, black-haired Peter—that was worst.
Then came a momentary silence, while
I listened for my footsteps as I went,
And loved my shekels, fondled them and laughed,
And then the storm: the shrieking and the groans,
The grinding and the lashing and the blood.
It brought some peace; and something of a thought
Took shape.—Oh! have you felt that cool desire,
That tender longing irresistible
For perfect silence? Never looking back,
I ran, and stopped, and, laughing ran again,
Close by the water fondly counted through
My shekels, firmly grasped them:—then the storm
Redoubled, as I hanged myself at last
To that sequestered tree beyond the lake.
        And first there was a torrent, then a sound
Like to the distant tolling of a bell
Heard through a wood at eventide, and then
A vision of the master clothed in white;
And then I stood, my shekels in my hand,
Without a change. (O God! O Providence
To grant desire, endurance, and through all
The promise of fulfilment!—While desire
Lives steadfast to its aim, death holds away.)

My land lies all about me, here the lake
And there the tree. I never see the moon.
I reckon not the passage of the hours;
And I am most content and fortunate,
Dreaming of wise prosperity to come."

He paused and cast a furtive glance, and I
Stood motionless in wonder, then began
To move because I feared him, but he wailed:
"You shall not take my shekels! You have come
To steal them from me. I am satisfied,
And so are all the people of the earth:
He is disproved who willed it otherwise,
For he was crucified and he is dead."
So saying, he began to count again
With hesitating voice and sideward looks,
Anxious towards the end, when fear began
To gather round the brilliance of his eyes,
And scarce had finished ere that tempest dire
Of human woe re-echoed from the world:
First shrieking of a hundred million slaves,
Then hopeless laughter hollow through the void,
Then tears of blood. A moment—and I felt
Those dreadful burning shekels in my hand,
And heard him clamour through the seething air:
"Perchance you come from Caiaphas the priest:
Tell him I hold my offer open yet!
Take him my shekels! You can save the world.
Cast them upon the pavement: leave them there!
And then shall be a miracle of joy,
And all the grinding of the wheels shall cease;
The shrieking and the laughter shall be stopped;
The blood shall flow no longer. Take them back!"
This uttering, he pressed me with his hands

As though to force me outward from my dream.
I, growing conscious of that other life
Which is not sleep, held fiercely in my grasp
Those burning shekels to redeem the world.
                    Thereon began the beating in my ears
Of time: but on the threshold of my sleep
That form of Judas haunted me again.
He wandered aimless underneath the grey,
And often stretched his empty hands aloft,
Groaning; and then—Oh! suddenly he came,
And, panting in an agony of speed,
Caught at my raiment, tearing with his nails,
And biting with his teeth upon my hand,
Till it relaxed. Then faintly I perceived
That dreadful form retreating through the grey,
Counting as in an ecstasy of greed.
His voice was like the grinding of the wheels:
And shivering in moonlight I awoke.

BIBLIOGRAPHY

VERSE

POEMS. *Elkin Mathews.* 1906.
JUDAS. *Sampson Low, Marston & Co. Ltd.* 1908.
BEFORE DAWN. *Constable.* 1911.
CHILDREN OF LOVE. *The Poetry Bookshop.* 1914.
TREES. *The Poetry Bookshop.* 1916.
STRANGE MEETINGS. *The Poetry Bookshop.* 1917.
REAL PROPERTY. *The Poetry Bookshop.* 1922.
SELECTION IN AUGUSTAN BOOKS OF POETRY. *Ernest Benn Ltd.*
   1927.
THE EARTH FOR SALE. *Chatto & Windus.* 1928.
THE WINTER SOLSTICE. *Faber & Faber Ltd.* 1928.
TWENTIETH CENTURY POETRY (ANTHOLOGY). *Chatto &
   Windus.* 1929.
ELM ANGEL. *Faber & Faber Ltd.* 1930.

PROSE

PROPOSALS FOR A VOLUNTARY NOBILITY. *Samurai Press.*
   1907.
THE EVOLUTION OF THE SOUL. *Samurai Press.* 1907.
THE CHRONICLE OF A PILGRIMAGE. (PARIS TO MILAN ON FOOT.)
   Sampson Low, Marston & Co. Ltd. 1909.
THE CHRONICLE OF A PILGRIMAGE. (PARIS TO MILAN ON FOOT.)
   Leonard Parsons Ltd. 1925.
SOME CONTEMPORARY POETS (1920). *Leonard Parsons Ltd.*
   1920.
SOME CONTEMPORARY POETS. *Simpkin Marshall Ltd.* 1928.
ONE DAY AWAKE. (MODERN MORALITY). *Poetry Bookshop.*
   1922.

INDEX TO FIRST LINES

215

216